Spring Into Life

How to Find True Acceptance after Your Mistakes

MICHELLE KLASEEN

Copyright © 2019 Michelle Klaseen
All rights reserved.

Printed in the United States of America

Published by Author Academy Elite
P.O. Box 43, Powell, OH 43035

www.AuthorAcademyElite.com

All rights reserved. No part of this publication may be reproduced, stored in a retrieval system, or transmitted in any form or by any means for example, electronic, photocopy, recording—without the prior written permission of the publisher. The only exception is brief quotations in printed reviews.

Paperback ISBN-978-1-64085-373-7

Hardcover ISBN-978-1-64085-374-4

Library of Congress Control Number: 2018952573

Every attempt has been made to protect the privacy of those who were involved in the narrative of this story. Details such as names, cities, references, and circumstances have been changed whenever possible. My life experiences and facts that are written are true to my words and my reactions without disrespect intended to anyone in the process.

Dedication

Thank you to my Father in Heaven who knows my heart and who has cared for and loved me more than I could have ever hoped or imagined. You have changed my life. Thank you for choosing me. To my husband, Ron, thank you for always encouraging me in all I do, and for believing in me when I didn't believe in myself. You are my special friend.

Contents

Part 1: Release and Forgive

1. Releasing the Pain Inside 1
2. Why Does This Happen to Me? 21
3. Why Do I Feel This Way? 39

Part 2: Ask and Believe

4. Searching for Love in All the Wrong Places . . . 51
5. Why Isn't God Doing Anything? 67
6. Letting Go of Anger 77

Part 3: Imagine and Choose

7. Transparency Brings Healing 93
8. Looking Beyond Self 107
9. Guarding Our Hearts From Hurt 117
10. Will I Ever Be Enough? 125
11. Whose Life Is This Anyway? 135
12. I Am Grateful for You 143
13. The Greatest Love Affair 151
14. About The Author 161

Introduction

Hi, thank you for investing in this book. God gave me a vision to write this book five years ago, and the symbolism of the book cover is amazing.

- Spring: renewal, new life, and a fresh start.
- The sunflower: fall, when everything falls off and dies, so it can become brand new in the spring. The sunflower also symbolizes- disciples (They follow the sun [Son] and are full of seeds [Word])[1]
- Purple Lilacs: Spirituality, first love and passion.[2]
- The color purple: is a symbol of royalty, power, ambition, peace and devotion.
- Blue: healing power of God
- Yellow: fire, purification, and the glory of God.[3]

I am writing this book because when I was going through all the chaos of my own life, I was searching for love and acceptance in all the wrong places. Telling God to back off because it was my life, and He wasn't going to interfere, and He did not. He loved me so much He let me do what I chose. As my life spiraled downward, it was if He would say, "Have you had enough?" Come to me my child, and I will give you rest from all of your self-inflicted pain. For my yoke is easy and my burden is light. (Matthew 11:30NKJV)

It is my hope that you will find life, hope and restoration in your own life by reading my story and what I have learned, and that you fall in love with Jesus along the way.

~Michelle~

Now the serpent was more cunning than any beast of the field which the Lord God had made. And he said to the woman, "Has God indeed said, 'You shall not eat of every tree of the garden'?" And the woman said to the serpent, "We may eat the fruit of the trees of the garden; but of the fruit of the tree which is in the midst of the garden, God has said, 'You shall not eat it, nor shall you touch it, lest you die. ' " Then the serpent said to the woman, "You will not surely die. For God knows that in the day you eat of it your eyes will be opened, and you will be like God, knowing good and evil."

—Genesis 3: 1–4 (NKJV)

CHAPTER 1

Releasing the Pain Inside

My life before Christ was not much different than when I accepted him into my heart. Life seemed to get worse in fact. Somehow I thought my relationship with Jesus would be remarkable, that I would immediately feel joy and happiness, and my whole life would be easy. That was not the case, however. I asked, "What am I doing wrong?"

My Father died when I was four, and I knew he went to heaven because that is where everyone says you go when you die. As a child, I wondered, "What is heaven? Who is God? Was He way up there in the sky somewhere?" Every time something went wrong, I'd look up to heaven and talk to my dad as if he were listening. Most of the time, it was in anger because he had left me and didn't give me any advice. I had to fend for myself, and that made me angry. I felt lost and alone, as I asked why he would do that to me.

I wondered, "Do I even need a father?" I have asked myself this question all of my life. Not having a father was the way it was. No one ever talked about him; he just was not there.

One day my world was shaken when my third-grade teacher leaned over and whispered in my ear, "I heard you're going to get a new dad and three new sisters." She sounded like it was supposed to be some exciting news in my life, but I felt my stomach do a flip-flop. I did not feel so happy about it. This man was going to take my mom away from me, and I knew it.

As I thought back to that night in the car, when my step dad proposed to my mom, I felt an ache in my heart; fear came over me. I had to share my mom with someone I didn't even know. I didn't want someone to take my place. What if she didn't have enough love for us all? I couldn't lose her too. It felt like she was choosing him and throwing me away. I was hoping it was a bad dream, but when my teacher spoke those words to me, I knew at that moment it was happening.

The weeks before the wedding we all did activities together as a family. He wasn't as bad as I thought he was going to be, although I was uncomfortable around him.

It was not familiar having a father figure in my life. But it also was fun having more kids to play with.

When they got married, it seemed like we were going to be one big happy family, and we liked to call ourselves the Brady Bunch. I felt like my new dad wanted me. One day, I felt special because he asked me to go for a ride with him and my three stepsisters—not my brother or sister. As we drove in the car that day, I looked up to see his beady eyes glaring at me in the rearview mirror. I felt a cold shiver run down my spine. It was a piercing glare, and I didn't feel comfortable anymore. I was confused as to why he was glaring at me and wondered what I had done wrong for him to look at me like that. I never found out, and I was never asked to go on a drive with him again.

As time went on, the silence and rejection hung in the air like a dark cloud. I'd test to see if my stepdad still liked me by mustering up the courage to say goodnight, as I descended the stairs to my bedroom. After I got up the courage to squeak out that word, there would be a long silence. He would finally say goodnight, and as time went on, he wouldn't respond at all. The question "What did I do wrong to make him not like me?" still swirled around in my head. I so badly wanted him to love and accept me, to treat me as his own.

During this time I began watching *Little House on the Prairie* and fell in love with Charles Ingalls, who was what I would call the perfect dad. If I could have chosen my dad, he would have been my choice. He was gentle and kind, and no matter what, he never made anyone feel stupid or got mad at them for making a mistake. I loved to imagine him as my dad and how life would be with such a sweet, gentle, kind man as he was tucking me in at night, kissing me on the forehead after giving me some great advice to help me feel better about something that was troubling me. I imagined myself as his daughter, I never missed an episode.

At the beginning of my eighth-grade year, we moved to my stepdad's ranch. My sister and I got the musty, cold, damp room with plaster coming off the walls while my stepsisters got the brand-new room upstairs with new carpet and new walls. Compared to the dungeon my sister and I had to stay in, it was beautiful, but we weren't allowed to go in their room. We weren't allowed to go down to the barnyard, but they could. They got to ride the horses; we didn't. They could sit in the living room and watch TV, but we couldn't. Whenever my stepdad would come in from outside, we were to go to our room and stay there.

When I'd answer the phone, and it was for him, I'd say, "Dad, it's for you." He would sit there and act like he didn't hear me say anything, staring straight forward until I left the room. Then he'd get up and answer the phone with a joyful, happy voice, one I'd never heard before. How I longed for him to speak that way to me.

We went to church every Sunday, no matter what. I didn't like it, but I knew if I didn't go, I was sure to go to hell when I died. Since I didn't want to burn in hell, I made sure to follow all the rules and be good. I'd say a prayer every night and ask for forgiveness for all the bad things I'd done so that I'd go to heaven if I happened to die before I woke up. I would think about God when I felt scared or needed something from Him or needed Him to get me out of a jam, but that was as far as I took my relationship with Him.

When I became interested in boys, I was excited for what God gave me and I would ask Him to keep me from doing what I wasn't supposed to. What I wanted to do and what God directed me to do were not the same, so I would choose what I wanted and thought I needed. I didn't believe God was on my side; I could see that from all of my experiences so far in my life to that point.

I became angry and confused about how my life was turning out. I'd take long walks and scream at my dad for dying and leaving me with an awful father. I blamed God for taking my dad from me and giving me a stepdad who didn't love me or take care of me. Why wasn't I good enough, pretty enough, or smart enough to be loved?

Everything I loved either died or left me. One day I made a pact with myself not to love anything or anyone. It hurt too much and all the circumstances in my life proved it. I was always feeling lost and alone, seeking and never finding that perfect romance that I thought would make everything better. I wanted to gaze into someone's eyes and know he was the one, trusting that he would never leave me or forsake me. I felt that aching—the yearning for someone to want me, to feel like I belonged to someone.

I love the story of Cinderella, in a lot of ways I felt like her. I got my idea of how romance was "suppose to" be by watching that movie over and over. Romance for me didn't ever end with a happy ending, it was always the other girl that got picked, I wasn't Cinderella after all. I didn't compare, was I actually the ugly step sister? I began to believe I wasn't good enough for anyone. Am I lovable?

The questions continued inside my head: *Why am I not perfect enough? What is wrong with me?* All the while I was asking, *If it was a lie I believed?* That I am forgiven, lovable, worthy of love, desirable, cherished, that my heart is good? It has taken me a lifetime of bumps, bruises, and heart-wrenching mistakes to figure out the answer. I listened to the lies that I told myself to justify my actions so that I could feel loved and accepted or to cover up my bad choices. I plotted, schemed, and knew what I was doing, but why? Was it because they said "If it feels good, do it?" Who are "they" anyway? With the excitement of every crush came a new sense of love and acceptance and the hope of being cherished and valued.

Insecure

At the end of my sixth-grade year, an upperclassman asked me to try out for the cheerleading squad, and she offered to make up my cheer and teach it to me. I talked my best friend Ellen into trying out with me. When I made the team and she did not, she got mad and wasn't my friend anymore. She didn't explain—she just stopped talking to me. This experience crushed me, but looking back, I learned if I succeed, then people hate me.

My freshman year of high school, Ellen and I became friends again. It was nice to have her back. Around that time I started going steady with Brian and we would all hang out together. When I couldn't be with Brian, he would take Ellen to town or to the movie, and afterward, they would come to visit me and tell me what a great time they had. I thought it was good that my two best friends got along so well. That was until one day when he broke up with me and started going steady with Ellen. I was devastated because he rejected me first. I was more upset because he wanted to end the relationship. To top it off—after a few weeks, he forbid Ellen to be my friend anymore. Once again I lost my best friend, and Brian had taken her from me.

That year when homecoming rolled around, I stayed at Rhonda's house a lot, she was one of my cheerleader buddies. She was a senior and I was a freshman. She looked like a Barbie doll, and I wanted to be just like her. Her mom was beautiful, sweet and she took me in as if I were her own. She'd call me "Missy," which made me feel special. She looked like Barbie too, and I told myself I was going to be like her when I grew up. Rhonda let me borrow her clothes, and she put makeup on me for the homecoming dance. I looked beautiful.

This was where I met my second boyfriend, Luke, and I thought he was the love of my life. He taught me everything I needed to know, told me everything I did wrong and helped me do things his way. He would point out things about other girls that he did not like. As far as physical features, he'd say, "See those creases under her butt cheeks? That is because she is fat. You'd better not let that happen." He liked me to be tan and skinny.

Luke and I dated all year, and when our junior-senior prom rolled around, he informed me he would not be taking me to the prom because he'd promised another girl he'd take her. Since he'd promised her before we started dating, he had to make good on his promise, so I agreed. After all, he loved me.

I served at the banquet that night, as we were cleaning up, the teachers told me to get my prom clothes on so I wouldn't be late for the grand march. When I told them I wasn't going and the reason why, they all opened their eyes wide and stared at me in disbelief. Listening to their comments, I thought maybe something wasn't quite right about what was going on. But I didn't want to mess up my relationship with Luke, and if I said something about it, I thought he might get mad at me and break up with me. I'd never had anyone love me like this before.

Luke had wanted to have sex with me all those months, but I had made a promise to myself that I wasn't going to do that. So I thought maybe that was the reason he didn't want to take me to prom. As I watched Luke and the other girl drive by the school, my heart felt heavy. I wondered if she was prettier or maybe a better person than I was. At any rate, she got to be with him and I didn't, so there had to be something wrong with me.

Luke broke up with me a few weeks later with no explanation, only demanding his class ring and his senior key back. I was devastated, but I had to do something and do it quick. A few weeks passed as I planned and schemed how to get him back.

I decided to have sex with him. Everyone else was doing it, and they seemed happy. God didn't strike them dead. So at age 14, I made the grownup decision to have sex. Afterward, I felt ashamed and embarrassed, but Luke assured me it was all right. He paid more attention to me after that, and it seemed as if he wanted me more, so at that time I thought it was all worth it. He left for college and would be back for homecoming to see me, but when he returned, I broke up with him. My heart had changed. I felt awful when he let me go without a fight, but a few months later he sent me a poster that said, "If you love something, let it go. If it comes back to you, it's yours. If it doesn't, it never was."

A few months later this very intriguing guy named Barrett came to school. He would talk dirty to me and tell me how desirable I was and how he wanted me. I would laugh him off, thinking, *you aren't ever going to get a piece of me.* Because everyone else wanted him, I wanted someone no one else would want. I was tired of getting thrown to the side.

One day my friend Rose, one of my cheerleader buddies, came up to me with a fascinating proposal. She said, "I think you should start going out with Barrett. I think he likes you, but he is messing around with Stephanie, and she is engaged to be married. You are the one person who I believe can make him stop." Wow! That was a shift in my favor: to think I could be the girl who could get the guy instead of getting the guy stolen from me. I took the challenge and went right to work. Within a month we were dating. We moved fast—sex on the first date—and he convinced me that smoking pot was all-natural and that it wouldn't hurt me. I was all in.

Barrett was the partying type—drinking, smoking—the kind who had to be around a lot of people. Our worlds didn't seem to fit together. He was so outgoing and mouthy, and he stood up for whatever he wanted. On the other hand, I was scared to drink and do drugs, but he convinced me it would be all right. His friends were guys he had beaten up. Barrett had a motto to beat up anyone who didn't think as he did, and after that, they would be friends. He had a way of convincing people that it was their fault and that they made him beat them.

During our first six months of dating, our relationship seemed rather unusual. Barrett wasn't around his friends when he was with me. When I'd ask him if he wanted to be with his friends, he'd always say no. After he would take me home, though, he'd go partying and hook up with other girls. I'd find out later. Even though I heard about it from the girls themselves, I didn't believe them because I thought I was the only one Barrett loved and they were jealous. He'd tell me those girls were only friends and had been for a long time. I believed him.

After a while, Barrett became possessive and abusive, and he would leave me at parties. When I'd ask him where he'd gone, he'd say that he went with some other girl to make a beer run or some other excuse. I'd buy into it since I wanted to believe I was the only one he cared about. Even his friends would tell me he was cheating on me and that I deserved better. But I wouldn't listen to them. I couldn't understand why everyone was against our relationship. I was so desperate for someone to love and accept me that I'd picture our situation in an entirely different light than it was.

One day Barrett and Stephanie left the school in her car. Barrett's friend Wyatt hurried to tell me about it and volunteered to chase them in his car so that I could catch them in the act. The act of what, I wasn't sure of, and I didn't want to believe all this was happening, even though I saw it with my own eyes. I joined Wyatt in the pursuit. It seemed like we were drag racing, chasing them around town. We were lucky we didn't end up hurt or get a speeding ticket. Eventually, Wyatt and I gave up the chase and went back to school.

When I asked Barrett about it later, of course, he lied. Not long after that, Stephanie and five of her friends circled me in front of the office at school and started yelling at me. It was the kind of bullying you see in the movies. I thought they were going to beat me. They were screaming that Barrett didn't want me and that he didn't even like me, saying things that are not worth repeating. I prayed that day, and later I recognized that God was watching over me. Those girls didn't lay a finger on me, and I felt as though I'd held my own reasonably well.

When I turned 15, I decided to move out of my mom's house on the ranch, I was tired of the rejection, and this was my opportunity to find happiness. I moved in with another family to be their nanny. I did as I pleased and became very independent, which Barrett did not like. We broke up for a time, but it wasn't long before he convinced me I couldn't live without him. The summer before my junior year in high school, I spent the three weeks before school with him in the mountains where we "played house." I loved pretending we were married, cooking for him and caring for him while he worked.

On the first day of school, he walked right past me when he got on the bus, not acknowledging me or sitting with me. I was devastated. I'd thought we were inseparable. How could he do that to me after I gave him everything? I let him know how I felt about that later, but again he convinced me I was ridiculous and that no one loved me the way he did and no one ever would.

If I wouldn't let him have sex with me, he'd say, "If you don't, someone else will." I hated that statement, and the thought of Barrett being with someone else drove me mad. I became controlling, full of anger and hostility. If he was talking to another girl in the hall and I saw it, suddenly it was as if no one else existed. I would scream "Barrett!" as I ran full speed ahead and jumped on him in a fit of rage. He would tell me how embarrassing I was and how everyone hated me. Whenever something didn't go my way or I didn't think he treated me the way he ought to, I'd scream and yell at him. All I wanted was love and acceptance, but I didn't know how to get it. I just knew how to throw a fit and get attention that way. I had done it all my life, and it seemed to work. Whenever Barrett and I would get in a knock-down fight, we would kiss and make up, and things would be better for a couple of weeks. Then the pattern would start over.

The fact that Barrett would be graduating soon and leaving me behind was more than I could handle. Again, I had to do something and do it right away, so I began to plan and scheme. As I look back, I realize my life was like a game of chess where I was always trying to figure out my opponent's next move. In Barrett's case, I made arrangements to move into his parents' house so I could be closer to him and control the situation better. I never said that out loud, nor did I recognize my motivations at the time. One problem with my plan was that I did not run it by Barrett. The day I moved in with his parents, he had already moved 45 miles away without telling me. I was shocked and mad. My plan was not working out as I'd thought it would.

When school started, I had gained twenty pounds. Since I couldn't fit into my clothes, I would wear Barrett's grease-stained work pants. I heard my classmates talking about how fat I'd gotten over the summer.

Life at Barrett's house wasn't what I thought it would be. His dad was an alcoholic and his mom a victim in her own home. I learned firsthand how to deal with an alcoholic and recognized what this kind of relationship was "supposed" to look like. I went from a dysfunctional home of silence to a dysfunctional home of yelling and cutting, hurtful words. I couldn't handle it anymore, so I moved in with a friend.

Since I thought I had to be skinny, I lived on coffee and started eating sugar-free fruit-flavored Certs. On rare occasions, I'd eat a can of green beans. If I ate too many, I'd make myself throw up. I also began to exercise and walk a lot, going from 140 pounds to 105 pounds. I was skinny, and I felt good—although when I'd look into the mirror, I was never thin enough.

During this time I started hanging out with the partiers at school instead of the jocks. The more independent I became, the more obsessed with me Barrett became. Finally, *I* was in control. I would meet Barrett at a party, get out of my car smoking a cigarette, he'd knock it out of my hand and tell me I was not allowed to smoke, and the fight was on.

One night I went to a party looking for Barrett. This night we had broken up (again), and I was heartbroken as usual. He was the love of my life. When he drove up, he was with Rose. He wouldn't talk to me, so I jumped in the back of his truck. He zoomed off and began doing donuts, making tight circles with his truck, gas pedal floored. I could have been thrown out, but I made my way to the back window and crawled in. He stopped the truck, got out, Rose also got out of the truck and asked me what was going on I explained to her about the fight we had. Of course, I was crying hysterically, as she assured me she was talking to him trying to help him feel better, she convinced me she was on my side. I trusted that she would fix our problem since she was the one who suggested I go out with him, so I got out peacefully and they drove off into the wilderness.

The next morning I set out to find Barrett. He was in the city park. He had his shirt off and had hickeys from his neck traveling all the way down his belly disappearing into his pants. When I asked about it, he assured me that it was done deliberately to make me mad. I begged him not to be mad at me and apologized over and over again. All I asked was that he'd take me back and love and accept me. It didn't matter how awful he was to me or how many times he cheated on me. I believed he loved me and that no one else could love me as he did. He beat that into me so many times that it became true for me. No one could tell me anything different.

Another time Barrett was mad at me was after he deserted me and I left a party with our friend, Henry. I thought it would be nice to see if Barrett noticed that I had gone for a change. When we got back into town, Barrett was racing around in his car looking for us. He was drunk and stopped in front of the truck. He went to the driver's door and grabbed the half-open window in a fit of rage, screaming, "Where have you been?" He then told Henry, "You don't "f***" with my woman." Then he shattered the window, spraying glass everywhere. He then punched Henry in the nose three times and took off walking across the school lawn.

I ran after him, pleading with him not to be mad and assuring him we hadn't been doing anything. He then swung around and struck me upside my head; I dropped to the ground and saw stars. I think he knocked me out for a brief moment, and when I could stand, I ran after him begging with him once again not to be mad and to please take me back. Of course, it ended the same way: we kissed, had sex, and made up. The cycle was always the same.

I had decided that after graduation I was going to break up with Barrett, leave town and never come back, but unfortunately, three days after graduation I was in a car accident. My two front teeth were knocked out when my face hit the steering wheel. I was furious. Barrett came to my rescue, I stayed at his parents' house. That night he didn't have the decency to let me rest. All he could think about was crawling on top of me and taking advantage of me again. But that was our relationship. That was how I knew he loved me. After I got some temporary teeth, he drove me to my new life. Once again, I said goodbye in hopes of never seeing him again.

A few weeks later I found out I was pregnant, so back into Barrett's arms I went. He promised he'd make everything right. I told myself I would not get married just because I was pregnant. We rented a trailer and started living together. Only he never came home, spending more time at the bar than he did with me. When Barrett would come home late at night, I'd scream and yell at him and ask where he'd been. He'd get mad and hit me and tell me to shut up.

I was offered a job washing dishes at the local diner, which I took and worked until the baby was born. Barrett then took a job out on the road traveling, working on microwave telephone towers along Interstate 70 across the United States. Once again, I was alone, and I went back to working as a dishwasher and waitress until the baby was older. When she was ten months old, I decided to leave Barrett. I was tired of being alone and didn't want to get yelled at or beaten anymore when he was home, so I moved to Boulder, Colorado with a friend and her husband and got a job waiting tables. After three weeks,

I felt I'd moved on. I had even started dating a guy. All in all, I loved my new life.

One night at 4 a.m., I couldn't sleep. I was up putting a puzzle together when there was a knock at the door. I knew who it was, but I hadn't told him where I'd gone. How did he find out? I opened the door, and there stood Barrett. My heart sank, and like a trained dog, I threw my arms around him as if I'd missed him and said, "I'm so glad to see you." It was a lie. I wasn't glad to see him.

For the next few days he clung to me like a magnet trying to convince me to go out on the road with him. He said I wouldn't have to cook or do my laundry, and I would be staying in hotels all the time. He was on a crew, and their wives were traveling with them so I'd have friends, and one of the women had a couple of children. He bought me gifts to show me how much money he was making. He made it sound so magical. How could I pass it up? I thought, *He did come all this way for me. Maybe it's a sign from God?* The thing that sealed the deal was that I was scared to tell him no. I knew he'd be mad at me if I refused to go. So I went.

After a few months, I got homesick. All I could think about was another guy whom I had only seen a couple of times. He had greeted me and smiled, so I thought he must be interested in me. I had to find out who he was and learn more about him. There I go again, plotting and scheming.

In the past, Barrett's dad had told me I couldn't stay at their house anymore unless we got married. Now Barrett told me he wouldn't fly me home unless we were married. I decided I could marry Barrett, and when I got back home I could get the marriage annulled, so I told Barrett, "we can get married."

His coworkers' wives were thrilled to help me with the wedding and helped me pick out a wedding dress and all the accessories. They agreed to babysit for us so we could have a wedding. We made arrangements with the justice of the peace. When we got to the courthouse, we hadn't brought any witnesses, so the judge took us to the town park where the town's annual ice-cream social was in full swing and there were plenty of witnesses. Our wedding was among strangers.

It was like playing a part in a drama. I got to act as if I were in a fairytale wedding, but in my mind, it was beginning to look like a nightmare. One lie led to another, but I kept up the game, not even being real with myself. I did earn my ticket home. After I got home, I started receiving gifts from people who had been at the ice cream social. We had made the front page of the local newspaper, and our address was printed for anyone who would like to send a card or gift. I couldn't let all those people down and have the marriage annulled. What would they think of me? Besides that, I wasn't sure how to do it anyway. I stayed married and continued the lie.

I started searching for "the other guy" I'd been fantasizing about. He would be my next way out: my knight in shining armor.

CHAPTER 2

Why Does This Happen to Me?

Deceived

Having been raised in the Christian church, I knew exactly what God said about adultery. I knew it was wrong, but thought maybe, just maybe, I could open up the Bible and find something that permitted me to be with a man who was not my husband. Surely, I had not read it correctly. After all, God loved me, and He knew my heart. He knew I had made a mistake marrying Barrett. I knew God would not tempt me beyond what I could handle. He knew I couldn't stay away from a man who paid attention to me, so He would never tempt me with such a situation. Since I thought of myself as a special case, I felt confident He would tell me it was OK to have an affair.

When I arrived home, I went in search of "the guy" who had said hello and smiled at me. I was determined to find love and acceptance, and I believed this was the person who could give me what I was looking for. His name was Neal. I believed God would not have put Neal in my path had He not wanted me to pursue a relationship with him. I believed I was justified to have an affair. After all I was in an abusive relationship, and this was my way out! I convinced myself that he was my knight in shining armor, and God sent him.

I went to my room and took my Bible off the shelf. I told God how much Neal meant to me and how badly I was in need of this relationship, so if He would please grant me this one request, I knew it would make me happy. I opened my Bible to the Ten Commandments and started reading down the list. "You shall have no other gods before Me. You shall not make for yourself a carved image. ... You shall not take the name of the Lord your God in vain. ... Remember the Sabbath day, to keep it holy... Honor your father and your mother... You shall not murder... You shall not commit adultery." There it was. I thought, "Wrong answer, God—I am out of here! This is my one chance to be happy. Besides, Neal is so good looking, and he wants me." I asked and received my answer, but I did not want to accept it. "What does God know anyway?" I arrogantly thought.

The choice to have an affair changed my life forever, yet the deliberate choice to disobey God and justify it disturbed me more than any other sin I could have committed. How could God love someone as corrupt as me? I was weighed down with blame, shame, and guilt.

On the outside, I looked as though I had it all together. Tan and physically fit, I looked successful, but on the inside I was like a decaying apple, rotting from the inside out. And I didn't know how to stop it.

I was so angry at myself for having had an affair and not being true to myself. I identified with what Paul says in Romans 7:16–20 (NKJV):

> If, then, I do what I will not to do, I agree with the law that *it is* good. But now, *it is* no longer I who do it, but sin that dwells in me. For I know that in me, (that is, in my flesh) nothing good dwells; for to will is present with me, but *how* to perform what is good I do not find. For the good that I will *to do*, I do not do, but the evil I will not *to do*, that I practice. Now if I do what I will not *to do*, it is no longer I who do it, but sin that dwells within me.

I chose to do what I'd told myself I would never do—have an affair, but I justified it because I'd entered into an abusive relationship with Barrett. I hated myself. I was furious and full of rage. If someone hit me or crossed me in any way, it was like uncorking a bottle, I would explode! I felt so much better when I could release all that pent-up anger by lashing out and screaming mean and hateful words to those around me. When I look back at all of the words that spewed from my mouth, I realize I was screaming them at myself.

After my fits of rage ended, the blame, shame, guilt, and self-condemnation would come, followed by days of crying, beating myself up, and replaying those words I'd heard over and over again: "You are ugly, screwed up; no one likes you, and everyone thinks you are crazy. You are an embarrassment. What is wrong with you? Are you retarded or something?"

In the beginning of our relationship, when the abuse first started, it was horrifying. I'd never had anyone hit me or say the things he would say. When the fight was over, he would apologize by saying, "I'm sorry you made me hit you. I love you. " As time went on, I didn't sit there and let him beat on me; I fought back. I learned abuse is never acceptable. When people would say, "Oh, you poor thing," I would feel guilty because of all the mind games Barrett had played when he told me I caused him to hit me. After all, it was my fault—that's what he told me over and over again. At the time, I didn't know what was true anymore.

After ten years of marriage and three children, we divorced.

I was deceived into believing that everything that happened to me was because of the choices I made, I did not recognize that, although I cannot control everything that happens to me, I am the only one who controls what I think and how I act. I was convinced it was my choices making other people treat me badly.

It didn't matter how tan, fit, or perfect I looked on the outside. When I looked in the mirror, all I saw was a fat, ugly, scared, screwed-up, miserable being. I was continually searching for the answers to be "normal," to love myself so that I could love another.

I would make myself so busy I didn't have time to deal with the pain. I found myself focused on all the things I did wrong and fell more deeply into insecurity, shame, blame, and guilt. I had so many things stacked up against me. How would I ever make it right? The people with whom I associated only confirmed how far I'd fallen and reinforced my belief that I was accused and declared guilty.

I felt pain in my heart from my father abandoning me and from my stepfather rejecting me, a fear of being alone, and depression because I was alone. I clung to all the happy moments I could remember, but I could only recall rejection and a feeling of being left with no one to love and accept me. I sought one man after another trying to fill that void of love and acceptance, only to end up with more rejection and even deeper feelings of blame, shame, and guilt.

I sought teachers, neighbors, classmates, and strangers, wondering if anyone would dare to love me. I could be anything they wanted me to be. If the relationship was not moving quickly enough or if individuals were not paying attention to me, I'd do whatever it took to start and sustain the relationship. After offering my heart and soul to so many men, I found out all they wanted was my body, and if they didn't act as if they desired me physically, then I thought I wasn't perfect enough. Always attracting men who were as needy as I was, I met a physical need but was left with an empty heart time after time. I thought that if only I had someone to love me, everything in my life would be perfect.

So many times I would begin to feel ugly and rejected because I believed only pretty girls got to be loved. I would set out to prove to myself I still measured up. I would go in search for someone to give me that validation. It could be a new acquaintance, someone who started paying attention to me, anyone who I thought might be interested in me. I would call them or seek them out, get into a conversation that would lead them to tell me how beautiful and how great a person I was.

If they didn't respond the way I thought they should—by coming on to me—I felt that there must be something wrong with me. I must not be pretty enough. If they took the bait, then I would feel beautiful, accepted, and loved … until I gave myself away. And then shame, blame, and guilt would return in an even stronger way as the cycle continued.

When I became involved in a healthy relationship with someone who didn't want to play games, I didn't know how to handle it. I would push for him to hit me because that was the only way I knew how to cope with disagreements. That's how I'd handled matters in my previous world. We did not release pent-up emotions through regular communication but by yelling, screaming, hitting, and using cutting words and getting all that anger out and putting it on another person. Somehow, it never worked. I felt worse when it was all over with even more shame, blame, and guilt.

I was deceiving myself in so many ways.

Breaking Free

Through counseling and reading, I believe God wants us to throw all our anger at Him so He, who began a good work, can bring it to completion (Philippians 1:6). When we want to lash out at someone, we do so because we feel we have a right to tell someone how we feel and let them know exactly where they went wrong. We think we are freeing ourselves and informing others, but actually, we are wounding ourselves as well as them. Only after we have spewed all that anger and those hurtful words out of our mouths do we realize we cannot take them back. We have already done the damage. It's like squeezing toothpaste out of the tube and then trying to put it back in. It's virtually impossible.

I have learned over the years that our words have creative power, and they work in both directions producing either positive or negative results. If we want blessings and benefits in our lives, we get to speak those qualities into our lives. It is never too late to start. Every time we mess up or say something we regret, we get to repent (change our mind) and start down a new path. Start today by speaking life over your situations; stop and think about what you want to say. We must ask ourselves, "Is what I'm about to say or do uplifting and encouraging to the person I am going to say it to?" We will not find ourselves having to apologize for our mistakes if we think about what we are doing beforehand and we avoid moving in a negative direction.

When we are cutting ourselves down, telling ourselves that we are failures, we are breaking our spirit. We are not building up our self-esteem nor loving ourselves. We can learn from our own mistakes, however. When we are truly sorry and regret what we have done, all one has to do is repent and decide not to do it again. We decide to be the people we want to be, envisioning ourselves as people who help others, including ourselves, to grow and create life.

Have you ever yelled at a child and seen how their little spirit shrinks as if it is drying up, but when you tell them how great they are, they grow, and their face brightens up? As adults, we are the same way. When we speak kind, wholesome words to ourselves, we light up and grow and bloom. On the other hand, perverse actions and negative talk bring us down, and we shrink inwardly. We feel depressed and would rather die than face another day. We start to dry up. Proverbs 15:4 NIV reminds us of this:

> The tongue that brings healing is a tree of life, but a deceitful tongue crushes the spirit.

Proverbs 12:18 repeats the NIV:

> Reckless words pierce like a sword, but the tongue of the wise brings healing.

Proverbs 16:24 NIV also has this to say:

> Pleasant words *are like* a honeycomb, sweetness to the soul and healing to the bones.

In summary, we can allow the Word to transform our soul.

John 10:10 NIV tells us the thief comes only to steal and kill and destroy; and he uses anything and anyone to distract us from the love of Jesus Christ. Have you ever noticed when you decide to do something good for someone else or decide to change something for the good, there is always something to distract you?

I can recall hearing all the voices in my head condemning me for all of the horrible things I'd done, knowing in my heart that they were wrong. I felt like there was no hope for me and that God would punish me for the rest of my life until I found this verse:

> *There is* therefore now no condemnation to those who are in Christ Jesus, who do not walk according to the flesh, but according to the Spirit.
>
> Romans 8:1(NKJV)

When we do something that we know is not good for us or we respond from a place of selfish motives, we call that "walking according to the flesh". When we only care about what we think or whenever we feel condemned or even if someone condemns us, this is a great indicator that God is not the one talking to us. God convicts us gently and lovingly and uses others to guide us gently back to a path of truth and love. He helps us break free.

A passage that has come to mean so much to me comes from John 8 where Jesus encounters a woman caught in the act of adultery, a woman with whom I identify. Here Jesus speaks of the scribes and Pharisees who brought this woman to Him as He was teaching and told Him what kind of woman she was and that they wanted to stone her. She knew what she had done. At one time, I identified with her—I pictured myself curled up in a ball on the ground waiting for that first stone to be hurled at me, anticipating the sting and every one that would follow. Jesus changed the atmosphere when He told the men, "He who is without sin among you cast the first stone." Amazingly, none of them could honestly say they had a life without sin. One by one, from the oldest to the youngest, they dropped their stones and walked away. And Jesus said to her, "Where are your accusers? Didn't even one of them condemn you?" She replied, "No, Lord." And He said, "Neither do I. Go and sin no more" (John 8:10–12 NLT).

Wow! He forgave her, and that spoke volumes to me. If the Lord forgave her, then surely, He had forgiven me also. I had stoned myself daily. I had been waiting for Him to reject me, to stone me Himself, but He never did. He loves me over and over again, yet I still continue to pick up that rock. I feel as though others pick up stones and hurl them at me. Maybe it has been my fault as I continue to bear the blame, shame, and guilt. I finally realized I was not receiving His forgiveness nor letting Him forgive me. I thought He needed to punish me, and if He were not going to do it, then I would punish myself. To receive forgiveness seemed too easy. In reality, it is that easy: we get to accept and believe. That's the beginning of breaking free.

For many years I couldn't forgive myself for what I had done and didn't understand how God could forgive me when I deliberately chose to commit adultery after He told me not to. I thought I was the only one who had ever committed such a horrific sin. Furthermore, I thought if I ever shared this with anyone or confessed it out loud, they would condemn me for sure.

Jesus came to this earth to show us how to live a sin-free life, and he suffered, having been tempted. He knew not to play around with the temptation but to rebuke it without sinning. All we have to do is turn away from whatever the temptation we may encounter. Hebrews 2:17–18 (NKJV) says this:

> Therefore, in all things He had to be made like *His* brethren, that He might be a merciful and faithful High Priest in things *pertaining* to God, to make propitiation for the sins of the people. For in that He Himself has suffered, being tempted. He is able to aid those who are tempted.

Hebrews 4:15(NKJV) reinforces the message about Jesus Christ:

> For we do not have a High Priest who cannot sympathize with our weaknesses, but was in all *points* tempted as *we are, yet* without sin.

For me, temptation started with wanting to date someone for all the wrong reasons. I entertained the thought, then I took action on the idea, and then the thought came to life. I did not rebuke that temptation but chose to go on the negative roller coaster ride that caused a lot of heartache and suffering in my life. Had I only responded to the temptation when I heard it, rebuked it, and then threw it out of my mind and not put any energy into it, my life would have turned out much differently.

Mark 11:23 speaks of any struggles we are having in our lives and shares how to proclaim that they are removed from our lives. That doesn't always mean the person or problem will go away, but it means we believe in what the Word says. We change and look at the issue that seems like a mountain in a whole new way, and somehow it goes away because we changed our thinking. We took the focus off of the problem and directed our thoughts on what Jesus would have done in this circumstance. We surrounded it with love, and it changed. Love is the answer to everything. God is love (1 John 4:8–11).

One of the sure ways to recognize if we are falling into temptation is to think we have to keep something a secret. I'm not talking about confidentiality. I'm talking about those relationships or behaviors that we think have to be kept undercover. When we have the thought of our spouse getting angry because we spoke to a particular individual or did or said something that wasn't quite right, that's when we get to ask ourselves, "Why am I keeping this a secret?" or "What is my true motive?"

I have to admit that I can justify anything to save my own skin. When I do that, it is a signal that a problem is arising. If I choose to go down that road, I will be trading in my freedom. We grieve our father God when we twist the Word to fit our needs, to condone our behavior, or to condemn another because of selfish ambition, greed, immorality, or power struggles in areas where we choose to engage.

> But the Helper, the Holy Spirit, whom the Father will send in My name, He will teach you all things, and bring your remembrance all that I said to you.
>
> —John 14:26 (NKJV)

The Holy Spirit will give us the wisdom to use the knowledge of the Word correctly. You can have all the knowledge in the world, but without the wisdom to put it to good use, it's just knowledge.

When we fully know that the act we are doing is wrong and still go ahead with it out of selfish ambition or for any other ungodly reason, this is sinning against God. Not only does it grieve Him, but this is when we open the door for shame, blame, guilt, resentment, anger … and the list goes on. It causes negative feelings toward ourselves that turn into self-hatred. It's a vicious, deadly cycle that steals, kills, and destroys everything around us.

I love James 1:13–15 where it talks about saying we are tempted by God, but the truth is God cannot be tempted by evil nor does He Himself tempt anyone. On the contrary, our own evil desires tempt us. Enticed by our desires, we entertain these ungodly thoughts. An example of a wicked way of thinking would be anything that does not line up with the Word of God. Any scheme to cause harm to another person, mentally, physically or socially, anything dishonest, or of that nature.

In my case, it was lusting after men and having thoughts about being with them, and then I put them into action because they looked so enticing and desirable in my own mind. I didn't think about all the evil or negative parts of that desire, only what looked good at the time. I now know if I had thought about the consequences and all the people involved, I might have changed my mind, but somehow when we are in that mindset of wanting what we want, the evil desires don't seem so evil at the time. We only want to fill our selfish void. Only after we look back at the situation can we see all the damage that has been done, primarily to ourselves.

The James passage gave me a greater understanding of the way I went about having an affair. I blamed it on God for dangling this man in front of me when, in fact, my own evil desires took me there. Jesus confronted temptation at all points, yet without sin—that is remarkable to me. The Word says we have the same ability to do just as Jesus did and more. Having a relationship with the Lord gives us the strength and the hope when those temptations come. We get to change our thinking immediately. We can ask him to help us change our thinking, confess and repent to Him, That's what it means to die to self—to let go of our own opinion and do as God would have us do. When we love the Lord God with all of our heart, mind, soul, and strength, we want to please Him and do well.

As we read the Ten Commandments if we choose to focus on the negatives that will be the direction we tend to go. When we keep our focus on loving God and our neighbor as ourselves Mark 12:29-31, the negatives in our life will start to diminish.

Exodus 20:1–2 NKJV, says this:

And God spoke all these words, saying: "I *am* the Lord your God, who brought you out of the land of Egypt, out of the house of bondage."

And then in Exodus 20:3–17, He clearly states what to stay away from in order to have all the fruits of the spirit. He loves us and wants us to live a long happy life that glorifies Him. It's the same thing as warning our children about dangerous circumstances, like not playing in the busy street.

When we make the choice to break any of the Ten Commandments, it's like getting stuck in a pit of quick sand; the more we try to get out in our own power the further bogged down we become. Jesus comes along and offers His hand to pull us out of the muck and the mire (bondage).

When we get out we get to choose to stay away from the pit's edge and focus on loving God with all our heart, mind, soul, strength and our neighbor as our self. That is where we find the fruit of the Spirit which is love, joy, peace, patience, kindness, goodness, faithfulness, gentleness, and self-control.

We can enjoy fruitful lives, all the fruit of the Spirit come with your salvation, having all the blessings and much more. If we have given our heart to Jesus, the Scripture says:

> But what does it say? *"The word is near you, in your mouth and in your heart,"* (that is, the word of faith which we preach): that if you confess with your mouth the Lord Jesus and believe in your heart that God has raised Him from the dead, you will be saved.
>
> —Romans 10:8-9 (NKJV).

Anything we want to improve is like exercise. We get to make the choice that we are going to practice, practice, and practice some more. When we make mistakes or fall back into the negative routine we have been practicing all our lives, we get back up, dust ourselves off, and look and see what didn't work and what did work. Finally, we ask ourselves how we can do things differently.

If we ask ourselves if we have offended someone or wronged them in any way, first of all, all one has to do is repent (change our mind). We then humble ourselves and apologize. The situation doesn't have to look a certain way. We can write a note, call the person on the phone, or get creative with the matter. Remember, because we apologize doesn't always mean we will get a positive response. We get to do our part and let God's healing salve do the rest. When we do this, we make it a priority to apologize for the wrong we've done. Striving to do the right thing keeps us accountable to ourselves. We are humbled by the experience because we don't like to admit when we're wrong. We are then more focused on how to improve our behavior, and more importantly, to be more aware of how we behave so that we can make that change. We then find the results are incredible.

After discovering these truths, I realized the destructive behavioral pattern I was experiencing over and over again stemmed from my feeling insecure and thinking I needed constant validation. I needed to hear I was on the right track, whether from a male friend, my husband, my mother, my children, or my boss. Moreover, I needed to feel loved and accepted, beautiful, smart, or well dressed. Now I realize I was always seeking man's approval, not God's. Confirmation doesn't come from man but from what Jesus Christ says we are and our receiving and believing its true and living our lives accordingly. Focusing on Jesus and His Word helps us to truly break free!

CHAPTER 3

Why Do I Feel This Way?

All my plans revolved around someone else. I needed someone else to be in my plans to take care of me. That was all I knew. I didn't know how to stop the lie of believing I didn't have what it took to make it on my own, or that "people" would be mad at me or that there would be no one else in the world to love me. I didn't want to be alone. I went along with pleasing everyone else by staying in a relationship that I knew was not healthy. It became more involved and more difficult to correct.

When I married Barrett, I was not following my heart. I was being led by what other people had said to me, by what I thought *they* wanted me to do. Of course, I did not want to disappoint anyone. If I chose not to stay married, a lot of people would be mad at me. I wondered what would be worse—being mad at myself or people being mad at me. At one time, people being mad at me was more important.

We do not have to keep making the same mistakes over and over again. So why do we? When we are worried what people will think or how can we can fix another person's problems because theirs seem so obvious and ours are too hard to figure out. We tend to think of ourselves as victims. How many times in your life have you looked at your circumstances and seen yourself as a victim with no way out? There seemed to be no other option.

Who told us that we didn't have a choice? We always get to choose. We get to ask our self, am I going to play victim to my circumstances or do something different? It's our choice. We hear it all the time: "I don't have a choice." We must realize there is always a choice. We are where we are today because of a decision we made. No one made them for us.

I chose to be in a relationship with an abusive person who was also an alcoholic. I chose to fight back. I chose to stay. He never tied me up. He never locked me up. I had plenty of opportunities to walk out whenever I wanted, but I chose to stay. It sounds crazy, but it was easier to stay and be abused than to be responsible and do something meaningful for me and my children. I was scared to be on my own and for my life to change. I was comfortable being able to come and go as I pleased, working out, walking, going to the lake, and lying on the beach. My husband Barrett sent the paycheck home, and I could play all the time. Staying was also easier because I didn't want to hurt his feelings or have his family hate me or think badly of me for getting divorced (which was against what God would want me to do).

The idea that God hates divorce and that I would go to hell if I got a divorce was part of my thinking. Staying in my situation was easier because Barrett was gone most of the time. He would be home one night and gone for two weeks. The money would come in, and I had no worries except when he came home. I thought I had it made, having my cake and eating it too. The longest he would stay at a time would be a couple of days.

In the meantime, I was seeking other men for companionship, value, love and acceptance. I didn't feel good about it, so one year, to justify my actions, I decided to keep a log of how much Barrett was actually around, and that made me feel better. After the year was over, he had been home a total of two months. As time went on and I continued to live a lie, I only became angrier and felt like a prisoner in my own skin. I put other people's opinion above what I actually wanted for myself.

Finally, I thought, *I can do it the way I've always done it and get the same results, or I can choose something different and get a different result.* Sometimes I chose the same behavior and realized later that I received the same results. It may have looked like a different choice with different circumstances, yet in the end, it was the same. We are the ones who get to learn to be responsible for our own decisions and stop blaming everyone else or the enemy for our circumstances. We are responsible since we make choices in the first place.

My Way

A great example of what I learned occurred when I chose to have an affair. It was not a spur-of-the-moment idea. I fed that evil desire for two years before it came to pass. I thought it through extensively. All Neal did was say hi to me and smile. I took that to mean he was interested in me. The fact that I was pregnant when this happened also made the situation more enticing because in my eyes I was fat and ugly, and a good-looking man was paying attention to me. I entertained that one greeting and created a story in my mind that he wanted a relationship with me. I would daydream about possibilities with him. I knew nothing about him, but I would plan to walk by when I saw him on the street.

After I'd had Barrett's baby, gotten married, and come home, I took it upon myself to actually stop my vehicle, roll down my window, and say to Neal, "Talk to me sometime." I was determined to create what I had imagined. I lied to family members about who he was and would tell them that he was a friend Barrett and I knew.

The devil is patient, sly, and devious. He loves for us to make mistakes, and he loves to put a wedge between us and God, yet he doesn't have to say much. Our evil desires take one of his suggestions that he whispers in our ear, and they make it look like a great opportunity in our favor, or it appears that we are missing out on something, and before you know it, we take it from there.

I wanted to be loved, respected, and cherished. I thought if I had the right man that all of my longing to be loved and accepted would be pacified because the man would provide this for me. Whenever I would begin to feel lonely, ugly, or not good enough, I would go in search of someone to fill that need to feel valued, accepted and cherished. Of course I didn't say to myself, "I need to go find someone to love me," but if someone was nice to me, I took it as a sign that they were interested in me.

If we can go back and think about the first time we felt neglected, rejected, or abandoned, the feeling we had will show up at similar times throughout our lives. Have you noticed that many of your circumstances seem to be the same, but they involve different people? There seems to be a pattern. I had a pattern of getting into relationships where I set them up to fail. I believed people were always betraying me, making promises to me, or acting as if they liked me. Something would happen, and before you knew it, they would be out of my life. Because in my mind, someone or something took them from me:

I wasn't pretty enough, smart enough, or thin enough, whatever the case might be.

The pattern of betrayal began when I was in first or second grade. We had an abundant cat population. My mom told me that a girl and her mom were coming to look at some of our kittens so she could take one home. I made my mom promise that she would not let the girl have my favorite kitten, Bunny. She could have any of the twenty cats we had, but not "Bunny." When I hurried home from school that day to play with my kitten, Bunny wasn't there. I was devastated. I ran to my mom and asked her where Bunny was. She had given her to the little girl. I asked my mom why she gave my kitten away when she promised me she would not. "Because the little girl wanted her," she told me. Bunny was mine, and my mom gave her away. What kind of little girl was this that my own mom thought she was more important than me? Was this girl cuter, sweeter, and more important? What was so great about this little girl that I didn't matter anymore? I was so hurt, but how I felt didn't matter.

It really wasn't about the cat—I felt that *I* wasn't important enough to matter. I felt that my mom loved her more than she loved me. I locked myself in the bathroom for hours and screamed, "I hate you!" over and over again until I was utterly exhausted. I did not come out of the bathroom until bedtime. After another hour of sobbing, Mom came in to try to make me feel better as she stroked my hair. I still couldn't believe she could do such a thing to me. I didn't want to accept her affection, but the love she gave caused me to soak it up. I can now see the pattern I created as I look back over my life and recall all the times when I misbehaved outrageously so I could receive love and acceptance.

Something within us shows that we were born to crave love, and we need it to survive. When we do not get love as a child or we do not learn what love is really about, we start creating whatever we need or think we need to fill us with love. If something works once for us to receive what we perceive as love, then we think that is the way to receive more love. Although I don't believe this occurs at a conscious level but on a subconscious level, we end up creating a habit to get our need met, whether a positive habit or a negative one. The unhealthy way of getting love always turns out to be a dead-end road leading to death: the death of self-esteem, death of a relationship, or a deep feeling of more loneliness and depression.

God's Way

If we are spending time with our creator, He will show us the truth. Even so, in exercising our freedom of will we get to choose whether we take God's advice and trust that He knows exactly what He is talking about or venture out on our own and do it our way.

God has promised to meet all of our needs according to His glorious riches. We all crave peace, so why do we worry, reason, feel selfish, and have unbelief when all of these concerns cause "anxiety"? All we get from those evil desires is rotten fruit. When God is in our decisions, peace comes with them. You know you are not doing what God wants for your life when you do not have peace. On the other hand, when you have love, joy, peace, patience, kindness, goodness, faithfulness, gentleness, and self-control, you know you are operating in the fruit of the Spirit. A great way to gauge what path you are on is to look at the fruit you are producing. Is it negative or positive? (Galatians 5:22-23)?

It all starts in our mind. When we are not continually renewing our mind when a thought comes in that isn't pleasing and is not from a place of love, it will not produce good fruit. Consequently, we must replace it. For example, what a man thinks is what he becomes. Are we speaking life or death to our self? It's finding something positive in what seems like a negative. Put a new meaning to all the past hurts you have encountered. This is how we renew our mind.

So when we accept Jesus as our personal Savior, we are in Christ, meaning everything we used to do, every sin habit we used to practice, is now forgiven. Since we made the choice to have Christ in our lives, we have also become a brand-new creation. That doesn't mean we won't be tempted to go back into the lifestyle we have known so well; we have practiced it so long. Rather, we have buried that old life in the grave. It's like the old person we once knew is now dead, and when we decide to accept Jesus in our lives, the old us—our former self—stays in the grave, and our new creation in Christ emerges.

Healing from our past wounds is similar to peeling back the layers of an onion—our former way of living is changed when we spend time in the living Word. It is also similar to a grasshopper, spider, or a snake: When they mature and develop more fully, they shed their old skin and produce new skin. The only difference is that it's still their skin. With our being a new creation, we grow from the inside out, not just our outer layer. God will guide us and talk to us and help us to become transformed into our beautiful, unique selves. We again get to make the choice to partner with God or not. The Scriptures tell us this:

> Therefore, if anyone *is* in Christ, he *is* a new creation; old things have passed away, behold, all things have become new.
>
> —2 Corinthians 5:17(NKJV)

We get to constantly remind ourselves, is this doing life my way or God's way?

Distractions

What are some of the distractions in your life holding you back from your greatness? So many obstacles distract us and attempt to keep us from becoming what we were created to be. When we are feeling a negative emotion or someone offends us, that is a distraction.

It takes time to understand and to give all the control of our lives to God. When we're trying to find the solution in our lives without God, we go in circles. The same decisions come up time and time again, and we make the same choices because we have not asked God what He thinks about what we are doing or what He thinks we ought to do. When we listen to God and He clearly tells us exactly how to proceed, we don't always trust Him to do it His way. So often we think our way is better, only because our way is familiar and requires no growth on our part. It's comfortable, and we know the routine well. It would save a lot of time and years if we'd do it His way from the beginning.

The Bible is the instruction manual for our lives. It tells us all we need to know to have a peaceful, abundant life. It tells how to accept Jesus as our personal Savior, and it shows us Jesus as the example to follow to gain peace in our lives. It tells who to forgive and shows how to forgive to have new life and how to speak to have an abundant life. All of these possibilities are in there.

> Therefore, as *the* elect of God, holy and beloved, put on tender mercies, kindness, humility, meekness, longsuffering, bearing with one another, and forgiving one another, if anyone has a complaint

against another; even as Christ forgave you, so you also *must do*.

—Colossians 3:12–13 (NKJV)

God has freely given us grace, so what are we waiting for? All one has to do is receive it. It is that easy: Accept the grace of God that He freely gives us. We get to receive it with gratitude instead of thinking we have to punish ourselves because we don't deserve it. Recognizing we don't deserve it makes what He has done for us even more beautiful, and it shows how much He really loves us. God loves us so much that He sent His one and only Son to be sin for us and to suffer for us so we could live a life free of guilt and shame.

When we spend time with God by reading and studying the Word, we will get to know Him, ask Him to speak to us through His word before we start to read. It's amazing the understanding that comes just by asking. He wants our heart, and He wants to have a relationship with us. In this whole world, He is the only one who can fill all those empty crevices we have been trying to fill with men/women, food, drugs and exercise…. You are complete in Him. Let Him love you, and you will not regret it.

CHAPTER 4
Searching for Love in All the Wrong Places

In the attempt to make myself feel, look, and be what I thought I should be, I attempted to resolve my issues and didn't include God. I convinced myself I had included Him because I occasionally opened up and talked to Him regarding a few situations. I decided since He wasn't stopping me, my behavior was acceptable. As a result, I became addicted in many different areas of my life, searching for love in all the wrong places as I tried to heal myself—heal or put together my self-improvement plan— but I wondered how a person as horrible as I had been could still be going to heaven.

Addiction comes about in various ways. Webster's Dictionary[4] defines the term this way: to devote or give (oneself) habitually or compulsively to something (e. g. caffeine or alcohol). As a noun, an addict is someone with an extreme need for something, especially narcotics. The term also refers to a devoted fan.

Sometimes life does not seem fair, and we want to blame God or someone else for all the wrong that is going on in our lives because we don't think we are doing anything wrong or are we? Do we go out with a girlfriend and gossip about someone and justify it because we are just seeking counsel from another friend? What is our true motive? Is it purely a selfish motivation? Only you know the answer to that question. If we are not sure and ask God to reveal our motive for doing it, He will let us know. Although we may not want to hear what He has to tell us and our first response will probably be denial with some anger with it, as we think about it, there is always an underlying motive we didn't even realize. God will always show us where the problem began in any situation.

Ask, seek, knock, and the door will open: the entrance to any answer you are seeking. We are never thrown into a situation without a way out, for God continually warns us. I have detected God's warning when I was about to do something that seemed to be an acceptable idea. I'll use the example of wanting to call a man who is not my husband. The first thing I want to do is hide or call in private. My first alert occurs when I start to dial his number. I notice an uneasy feeling in my stomach, and I begin to shake. I tell myself I'm just nervous, but it is my alarm (the Holy Spirit) telling me there is danger ahead. I shrug it off and proceed, but there is absolutely no peace. Each time I decide to go against the Holy Spirit's warning, I become immune to His prompting, and soon I don't hear Him anymore.

We always have a choice. The question remains, "Are we listening?" We can become so distracted by everything going on in our lives. The internet and everything associated with it becomes a great distraction, not to mention an addiction. We can become addicted to work, food, people, exercise—so many areas of life not only become addictions but become idols. Such distractions interfere with our relationship with our Heavenly Father. We encounter experiences that may lead to being addicted, but God warns us. It's the way God designed us. He wants our heart, and He wants us to become "addicted" to Him.

> No temptation has overtaken you except such as is common to man; but God *is* faithful, who will not allow you to be tempted beyond what you are able, but with the temptation will also make the way of escape, that you may be able to bear *it*.
>
> —1 Corinthians 10:13 (NKJV)

In the past when I was in search of value, love and acceptance I would seek different situations involving addiction to find what I was looking for. I became addicted to false satisfaction which led to frustration, and I found that these actions and substances began to control my thinking and my life. I felt like I was in a trap trying to find more of something, I didn't know what it was.

Smoking

One day, for whatever reason, I decided I was going to start smoking. I was with a friend who wanted me to try it out because she smoked and wanted some company, so she would feel better about smoking. Although she never said that, I now know that was the case. I felt like she would accept me as a friend if I smoked with her, if I refused she wouldn't like me.

As we lit up that first time, I had a feeling in my gut that I should not be doing this. That was the Holy Spirit warning me, but I put the cigarette up to my lips and took a significant drag, inhaled deeply, and immediately started coughing uncontrollably. I felt as though I would cough up my lungs.

That response indicated some foreign substance had just entered my body, which was rejecting it and doing everything to get rid of it. I may have even become ill from it, but then I decided it wasn't so bad after all. The more I smoked, the better it seemed, and after a while I didn't get lightheaded anymore. I stopped noticing that gut feeling asking if I should be doing this. My body became used to it and then began to crave that substance, and I felt at that time as though I had to have it to be happy.

That little white roll of leaves started to control my life. I couldn't leave home without it. I planned my day around it to make sure it always came with me. In the past cigarettes had become a burden for me. I had been smoking for years and now wanted to quit, but when I'd start to quit, something had this hold on me. I couldn't stop thinking about smoking, and I thought I was in need of it. I thought it made me happy, and if I didn't have it, I became angry. How could it be good if it caused such turmoil within me? So quitting had become somewhat more difficult, but I chose to stop smoking and went through the phase of something dying and grieving for it. I went through this painful process, and replaced it with another horrible addiction.

Comfort Food

Food is everywhere, and oh, how it makes me feel good! Everyone has different reasons for reaching for the fork. Sometimes I don't even need a fork. I want to devour that piece of chocolate cake, the candy bar, the bag of chips, and the list goes on. Food has become a pacifier providing a false, calming reality. I think I will feel better, but based on past experiences, I know when I eat a piece of cake I will then say, "What the heck—I'll start my diet tomorrow." Later, I follow with "I'll just eat the whole thing to get it out of the house." I will then get bloated, or I may get a headache, diarrhea, and of course, gain five pounds. Now that I think about it, does that cake make me feel better? It seems to pacify something as it goes down, but there is still that aching for something more. *Maybe I need something salty instead? Perhaps I'm just thirsty....*

Searching for something to fill the void inside, I step on the scale to see if what I ate made me fat. I stare down at the number and let it dictate if I am worthy or not. At that point, not only have I put on weight, but my energy level is also low. My joints start to ache. Those are all warning signs that eating and overindulging with food is not good for me.

According to *A More Excellent Way* by Henry W. Wright[5], overeating can be triggered by the fear of rejection, fear of man, fear of failure, and fear of abandonment. What am I searching for when I indulge in comfort food? For years, I didn't realize the food didn't fill the void in my heart. So I'd turn to or add another solution to see if that met the need.

Weighing Myself

Hearing others make fun of overweight people and hearing people talk about gaining weight used to trigger deep insecurity and fear of rejection in me. For example, if I felt as though I needed to lose weight, and I needed to do it quickly. As a result, the scales became my judge as to whether or not I was worthy of eating or not. I would punish myself and not let myself eat unless the scale said what I thought it ought to say. When I'd weigh myself, if the scale did not show my ideal weight or under, then I'd feel depressed, punish myself by not eating, and tell myself I was not allowed to eat anything unless someone offered it to me. In another instance, if I had to open a cupboard or unwrap the food, I couldn't have it. The number on the scale dictated if I had been good or bad. I'd weigh myself every morning, noon, and night, in hopes that I hadn't gained any weight, revealing I was thin enough.

Bulimia

Because of self-hatred, self-rejection, and the guilt I felt not having control in my life, I began consuming abnormally large quantities of food in a short time. To avoid gaining weight, which aggravated the situation, I found myself throwing up what I had consumed, indicating a psychological disorder called bulimia. At the time, I remembered hearing about an extremely underweight girl who was called bulimic. I thought I could try stuffing myself with too much food and then throwing it up a few times, and then I would stop. It seemed like a great idea, and the idea intrigued me. I could eat anything I want to, throw it up, and never gain weight. As I began the process, I started losing weight, and everyone was noticing how good I looked. When I would look in the mirror, however, all I saw was a fat, frumpy girl. Soon I became addicted to the process and decided it was necessary to stay thin. When I started feeling bad, my body said "no more", but the need to remain ultra slim and to feel fulfilled was stronger. I felt that by being super slim I'd get more love and acceptance.

I was never satisfied with my body, and when I looked in the mirror, it didn't matter how thin I was or how beautiful I looked, there was still something missing. What was it? I would hear people tease others or make jokes about being fat, and no way did I want anyone to tease me. I'd gorge myself with whatever I could get my hands on in hopes that for a little while it would satisfy my craving and fill that huge void I was feeling. Afterward, I felt bloated and became angry with myself for not having any self-control. The guilt would then come, along with the punishment. I had to go throw up everything I had just eaten. I thought I could not gain any weight or people wouldn't like me.

Anorexic

During this turbulent period of my life, I encountered another severe eating disorder: anorexia. I became obsessed with a desire to lose weight by refusing to eat. Because of this behavior, I felt controlled, tormented, and isolated. I started pretending and lying. For example, I told people I had already eaten before I came to their house, or I couldn't go to dinner parties because of the kids, or I was sick, and the list went on and on.

To me, everyone seemed slim, trim, and well put together, and I compared myself with everyone and believed I needed to be thinner to be loved and accepted. I felt powerful by not eating. Once I'd started to eat, I couldn't stop. I felt like an alcoholic who went on a binge after not drinking for a long time. When I overindulged, I'd revert to throwing up or taking a laxative.

Exercise

On New Year's Eve when I was sixteen, I was babysitting and watching the ball drop from Times Square on TV. On that night, I made a New Year's resolution that I would exercise for the rest of my life, and it's the only New Year's resolution I have ever kept.

At that time, I never thought exercise could be addictive. I considered trading in my other unhealthy habits for a positive one—this would be an excellent habit to create for all the right reasons. I had gained the 20 pounds in high school because I wasn't as active as I had been when cheerleading. My mom had taught me that if I burned off more calories than I took in, I would lose weight.

The boys in my class told me how upset they were at me because I didn't try out for cheerleading, and now the school had fat girls for cheerleaders. That spoke volumes to me because I didn't want to be one of those fat girls, but I was. I felt as if everyone had expectations of me, and I had to meet their expectations, or they would not like me.

When I found that the pounds were not coming off quickly enough, I had to do more. I remembered when I had to walk one to two miles to the bus every day; some of the boys on the bus would comment about how I'd never become fat because I had to walk so far. All those comments people would make I tucked away in my mind. One of the commercials that stuck in my head was "You are what you eat, so you better eat light," said the Wishbone Italian dressing commercial. All of these statements were the answers to my problems, so I thought. I began to walk again. I maintained my 105 weight. I felt proud when people whispered, and I believed they were jealous because I looked so good.

After I graduated and found out I was pregnant, I began to eat a more balanced diet, but I continued to exercise. After I had my baby and found that the weight wasn't coming off soon enough, I stopped eating and kept nursing and exercising, and I lost the weight quickly. I was lean but felt that if I missed one day of exercise I'd gain the weight I'd lost. I believed I could feel it growing on me if I didn't exercise.

I had a particular time every day to exercise. Consistent exercise seemed to be the only factor with positive results that I could control. If anyone tried to get in the way of my workouts or if I missed a day, I was like a time bomb going off. I inevitably exploded into a hateful and mean individual. Since I had so much pent up energy, anger, and resentment, I needed something to make me feel better—to keep all the energy, both positive and negative, at bay. Rigorous exercise helped me exhaust the anger I felt inside. It was another form of punishing myself for overeating. I had to stay busy so that I didn't have time to think about anything. I could not sit still for even five minutes. I was always trying to make all the pain go away by making my body perfect. Even though I had improved in my physical conditioning, I couldn't see it, and it wasn't enough. Nothing had ever been enough.

I'd get considerable attention for being in excellent shape. Men especially paid attention to me, and before I knew it, exercise had become my idol. I also increased my walking. I'd load my children in the stroller and walk for miles. I got the name "The Walking Girl." I loved all of the attention I received because I walked so much. Everyone would comment on how vibrant I looked and how buff I was, so exercise became another idol because I gained considerable attention.

Having Babies

Having babies also became an addiction for me. The moment I had my first child and the doctor placed her on my stomach, I had never felt a love so bonding and beautiful. That kind of love was something I had longed for all my life. It was incredible to have this human being love me, cherish me, and look to me for her every need.

Most importantly, she returned my love, and it didn't matter what I looked like or the way I conducted myself—she loved me. It was the most satisfying feeling ever.

My children became my life, and I didn't feel confident when they weren't with me. I hid behind them. They were my confidence, my reason for everything I did. They became another idol because I looked to them for my confidence, love, support, value and confirmation that I was acceptable.

By the time my first child reached the age of four, I had a novel idea: I needed another baby. I justified the idea, first by thinking I needed to lose weight. I felt I had started gaining weight and didn't have a grip on the situation, so having a baby was the *answer*. I was sure I'd gain weight for nine months, but then when I started nursing, I'd be thin again. Babies are fat suckers since the fat in a pregnant woman's body turns to milk. Infants digest it, and the more they eat, the thinner you become.

Having an additional child could also result in receiving more love. I could create a world around me where everyone loves me, so that's what I did. They were the best friends I'd ever had, yet they too became idols. Children are unusual because they love you no matter what.

Suntan

Oh, how I love the sun! When I was ten, I started taking swimming lessons, and having a tan brought attention to me. I knew nothing about being tan until one day when my mom was having a meeting at our house, and when I got home, the women at the gathering kept commenting about how tan I was. They'd tell me, "You're brown as a berry" and "You look beautiful!" What they said stuck with me.

From that time on, I started lying in the sun. I told myself I needed a tan for people to love and accept me. So every year, I put that expectation on myself because I thought that's what people expected of me, and I thought I had to please people.

After I entered high school, people would warn me that the sun was not good for my skin. One woman showed me how it damaged her skin. Since she was beautiful, I didn't care. Was she holding some secret back from me? I loved to be tan. It was my ticket for people to admire me. And it made me feel good. I received much attention for being fit and tan, yet there was still something missing. The sun too had become one more idol.

Men

I continued to yearn for love and acceptance; most of all I was seeking validation that I was lovable and that someone would cherish me. I'd begun to feel depressed and lonely, and I noticed whenever I was feeling at my lowest point or when I'd least expect it, a man would pay me a compliment. At first, I thought it was funny, or they were joking around, and I'd try to ignore their comments. Then they'd give me more attention, and I'd start to take notice and feel as if they must be interested in me. I'd change the way I would dress when I'd go for a walk or go to work. I'd start feeling lighthearted and sexy again from the addiction to attention and compliments. It would make me feel as if I did matter, that I did have a purpose. Their words and gestures made me feel alive again when I thought I had nothing more to live for nor anyone to impress.

I thought each man I encountered was the answer to fill the void of this need for love, acceptance, and the yearning to know that I was desirable. I would live for that one second of eye contact, magnify it in my mind, and interpret it to mean he wanted to have a relationship with me. Then one day I'd take it one step further and get his number. The Holy Spirit would give me that nudge not to, but I'd get the number anyway. I experienced the thrill of the secret romance trying to fill the ache I still had inside, the emptiness. One more idol surfaced as I was seeking validation from man instead of God.

Why do we get addicted to all these different aspects of life that give us false illusions of self-worth? I believe this intense pursuit is due to a search for a relationship. God created us for relationship, and the ultimate relationship that brings joy, peace, patience, kindness, and everything we need is to give our heart, mind, and soul to the Lord Jesus Christ and seek Him for everything. He satisfies, and it's through our relationship with Him that we become so fulfilled we no longer feel the need to look elsewhere.

When we start to reach for that piece of cake or seek one of the other habits we have created to make ourselves feel better, we ought to ask, "What am I feeling?" We ought to sit down with a tall glass of water, open our Bible, and ask God to fill us and to speak to us through His Word, and He will cover us with His grace and mercy. We will realize we do not need to crave anything but Him if we practice developing this new habit instead of trying one of the other methods we have been practicing.

If we slip back into a bad habit or fail in our efforts one day, that's okay. We get to repent and start over, and we keep practicing. Soon we will notice we aren't even thinking about whatever took us off course.

Something else we can do is pick a verse out of the Bible, a passage that speaks to us. We can write it on a sheet of paper or an index card and keep it in our pocket until we have it memorized. Every time that unwanted feeling surfaces, we can say the verse over and over again until we feel ourselves shift into peace.

Here is one of my favorites:

Be anxious for nothing, but in everything by prayer and supplication, with thanksgiving, let your requests be made known to God; and the peace of God, which surpasses all understanding, will guard your hearts and minds through Christ Jesus.

—Philippians 4:6–7 (NKJV)

Once we receive Jesus as our personal savior, nothing can separate us from His love (Romans 8:37–39). He loves us unconditionally, and He has forgiven all our sins past, present, and future. He loves us no matter what. As our relationship with Him gets stronger, we will not want to do anything that would grieve Him because we love Him that much.

CHAPTER 5

Why Isn't God Doing Anything?

For God has not given us a spirit of fear, but of power and of love and of a sound mind.

—2 Timothy 1:7 (NKJV)

I couldn't figure out the source of all the torment in my mind. I was so mentally tortured that I didn't like going anywhere with my husband Barrett for fear someone would approach him in an inappropriate way or that he would be interested in someone else. Then again, I thought maybe someone would know what mistakes I had made and tell him. These fears came from my guilty conscience since I knew all the mistakes I had made and knew everyone else could see them on my face or in my actions. I didn't think anyone could be as deceptive and underhanded as I had been, and I believed I wasn't good enough, pretty enough, or worthy enough to be happy. I deserved to be punished. I believed that God put different people in my life to pay me back for all that I did. I was waiting for God to do something to me, not realizing He had always only loved me.

Because of my attitude toward the sins I had committed, I thought my husband Barrett felt as I did. For example, when we would go to a social event, I would scan the room, comparing myself to other women. If I felt any of the women were prettier than I was or if I saw him looking in a certain direction and there was a woman standing there, she became the target. I felt as if he was looking for someone more attractive, and I would watch her the whole time we were there. I was the one creating the drama in my mind. To make things worse, I'd accuse him of watching her and desiring her. This situation kept spiraling downward until both of us were having such a miserable time we would leave, because of the torment I created in my mind when I thought he wanted to leave me for someone else. In reality, I was entertaining unhealthy thoughts and acting on them. I was considering the possibility that he would be unfaithful because I had been unfaithful so many times before.

I was afraid my husband would find someone more attractive and prefer being with her instead of me. I would get so worked up that I hated going anywhere. I didn't think I could control my thoughts. I believed the lie that I was not worthy to be loved by anyone because my thinking was unclear, still full of shame, blame, and guilt. I hadn't forgiven myself. I felt I deserved more punishment for my sins, even though Jesus died and took care of all of that for me. I didn't understand that enormous act of love when God sent His Son as the ultimate sacrifice for all of our sins: past, present, and future.

I became frustrated, I didn't understand why God wasn't doing anything. If something in my life did not turn out the way I thought it should, for example; asking to have a different man in my life, I didn't listen to Him when He showed me Truth, I convinced myself that having another relationship was God's will. Although He clearly did not give me the go ahead. I decided what I wanted to do and expected Him to bless the situation. I went back and compared the Word to what I thought I heard Him say, and He showed me where I had decided to take over and do things my way.

Jesus said, "Come follow Me," and I accepted. But on my terms. When life started to get hard and I didn't understand my relationship with Him, I put limits on God. I would tell Him what I wanted. I didn't want to stop doing the things I liked to do, or change my ways. I thought the Christian life was boring. As I questioned God, I decided to put my relationship with Him on hold. I wanted to "live a little" and do the things I wanted to do, I would follow Him when I got older. There is plenty of time.

It was not easy when I accepted Christ into my life and chose to turn from my life of sin and start walking with God. All of a sudden, situations were more difficult to figure out as more opportunities to follow the Word of God were presented to me. The more I read my Bible, the more I seemed to be tempted, or I had more difficulty in every area of my life. I would decide to stop a bad habit or start a new diet. When I focused on what I couldn't have, I wanted to do it more than I did before I decided I wasn't going to do it anymore.

Someone once said, "You can't avoid a *don't*."

I had to decide to believe what His Word says about me and who He created me to be instead of all the lies I had told myself throughout my life. When I do listen to the Father and believe what He says, I find He is faithful, just as He says He is. His promises are true He does not change like shifting shadows, according to James 1:17.

The Word clearly states:

Therefore, if anyone is in Christ, *he is* a new creation, old things have passed away; behold, all things have become new.

—2 Corinthians 5:17(NKJV)

It does not indicate this individual might be made new in the future—the born-again believer is already a new creation. There is no question about identity. The old has already passed away and *all things have become new*, not some things but *all* things. When we decide to follow Jesus, we ask Him to forgive us, and He does. The Scriptures tell us:

> "No more shall every man teach his neighbor, and every man his brother, saying, 'Know the Lord,' for they all shall know Me, from the least of them to the greatest of them, says the Lord. For I will forgive their iniquity, and their sin I will remember no more."
>
> —Jeremiah 31:34 (NKJV)

> "If you love Me, keep My commandments. [The 1st and greatest commandment is to Love the Lord God with all your heart, mind, soul and strength and the 2nd is like it, to love your neighbor as yourself] And I will pray the Father, and He will give you another Helper, that He may abide with you forever—the Spirit of truth, whom the world cannot receive, because it neither sees Him nor knows Him; but you know Him, for He dwells with you and will be in you.
>
> —John 14:15–17 (NKJV)

As I started studying the scriptures I realized I was either serving God or serving Satan and my fleshly desires, there was no in between. It was either yes or no: God's way or my flawed way.

All my life, I believed the Ten Commandments said "don't do this" and "don't do that." How challenging was that? Exodus 20:1 is meant to help us stay out of bondage and to keep us from creating our own heartache. We should stay away from these practices as the Ten Commandments instruct us. Later in Scripture, however, the two greatest commandments tell us to love the Lord God with all our heart, mind, soul, and strength and to love our neighbor as ourselves.

Remember, the Devil does not want us to live for Jesus; he wants us to keep wallowing in sin. Before we accepted Jesus as our Savior, the Devil didn't have to worry about us. We were no threat to him. Now that we have accepted Jesus as Savior, he wants to convince us that Jesus isn't all He says He is and wants to convince us that we are beyond help. It's all a lie. Joyce Meyer says we have to become stronger and resist the Devil's attempts to keep us from pushing through to the other side, no matter how difficult it seems.[6]

The Holy Spirit is in us, guiding us into all truth. As we read God's Word and learn all the revelations about His character, we will recognize when the Devil is lying to us. It's similar to handling real money every day. When a counterfeit comes through, we can identify it right away if we know what the real thing is like. When we are in the Word every day, we will recognize Satan's lies because we will know the truth. If we feel afraid, remember fear is a liar, and *perfect* love casts out fear (1John 4:18).

"Draw near to God, and He will draw near to you," James 4:8 tells us. We get to respond to what God has called us to do. If He has asked us to let go of a bad habit or inappropriate behavior, we get to listen to what He says and trust His discernment. We cannot graduate to the next level.

As I developed and matured, I thought of my struggles as accomplishments when I conquered them. It was interesting how the same struggles showed up time and time again, yet they looked somewhat different every time. If I focused on the struggle, I continually asked God, "Why did that happen to me?" All the while, He was telling me to focus on Him, to focus on loving Him. When it finally dawned on me what was happening, I caught myself in the middle of the circumstance and corrected it (with God's help, of course), and then I felt as though I got to graduate to the next level of understanding God.

God was with me and had been with me the whole time. The Scripture tells us:

> *Let your conduct* be without covetousness, *be* content with such things as you have. For He Himself has said, "*I will never leave you nor forsake you.*" So

we may boldly say: *"The Lord is my helper; I will not fear. What can man do to me?"*

—Hebrews 13:5-7 (NKJV)

He was being a gentleman and would not interfere with my free will. When I chose fear over His love, I chose to be miserable. When I surrendered to His truth and did not entertain all of those negative thoughts and feelings, then He was able to help me through the situation and the fear I felt. He brought to remembrances all of His truth He had been teaching me through the Word. It was not an easy road to travel to stop all the bad habits I created for myself when I tried to protect myself from everyone. This behavior caused nothing but torment for me. As Joyce Meyers said, "To overcome the habit you have created you have to stop yourself in the middle of it."[7] This statement also led to another story of surrender.

When I was married to Barrett, he went to the bar every night, while I lay in bed and became more and more upset. I'd torment myself with entertaining thoughts of him being with someone else. Now I found myself in my second marriage, and because I'd practiced that habit for so long, it carried over into my relationship with Neo. I became so possessive I didn't want him ever going out in the evening.

On one particular night, he had a meeting. I had been listening to Joyce Meyer's teachings so that I could get God's truth in me and practice what the Word says. Time passed, and later that night all those feelings I previously had started flooding my mind the later it got. Whenever a negative thought would come to mind, I would cry out to God and ask Him to help me. I cried and started sweating and sobbing as I let God's love wash over me. I surrendered all of my hurt and pain and gave it to Him. It was one of the most difficult challenges I have ever faced. When my husband came to bed, instead of accusing him and feeling like I wanted to rip his head off, I had a peace that surpassed all understanding. That is how God helps us, when we trust Him with our hurt, and tell Him about what we are feeling and how it is affecting us. As we feel the pain His truth comes to our remembrance, and washes over us. We have to let go of the way we see the situation, surrender and let Him put his healing salve all around us. We must trust that He will because He says He will. His promises are true and trustworthy, and He can't lie. He has made a covenant with us. (Titus 1:2, Hebrews 8:7-13)

The Scripture tells us:

> As you therefore have received Christ Jesus the Lord, so walk in Him, rooted and built up in

Him and established in the faith, as you have been taught, abounding in it with thanksgiving. Beware lest anyone cheat you through philosophy and empty deceit, according to the tradition of men, according to the basic principles of the world, and not according to Christ.

—Colossians 2:6–8 (NKJV)

Jesus Christ *is* the same yesterday, today, and forever.

—Hebrews 13:8 (NKJV)

For all the promises of God in Him *are* Yes, and in Him Amen, to the glory of God through us. Now He who establishes us with you in Christ and has anointed us *is* God, who has also sealed us and given us the Spirit in our hearts as a guarantee.

—2 Corinthians 1:20–22 (NKJV)

Reading and Studying the Word has shown me that God has been growing me and changing me, as He loved me through every situation. At the time I couldn't see that He was doing anything, but as I look back at my life I see how He has done everything to carry me through.

CHAPTER 6

Letting Go of Anger

When we accept Jesus as our personal Savior, we become a new creation. Do we change at that moment? Yes, we have made the choice to be different. We have decided we are tired of getting what we've always received; therefore, the love of Jesus has drawn us to become something better. At that moment, we have chosen to behave differently in order to improve our lives. Every time the old routine comes up—anger, greed, lying, cheating, drinking, smoking, or whatever it is—that is the "old us." We go back to past old behavior because it is comfortable, familiar, and we've learned how to self-protect by operating in our old patterns. We know how to live in that skin, but because we have chosen to be different, the work has just begun. It's time to walk the walk, in other words, to act the way that agrees with the things we say.

This Scripture gives a great example:

> Does a spring send forth fresh *water* and bitter from the same opening? Can a fig tree, my brethren, bear olives, or a grapevine bear figs? Thus no spring yields both salt water and fresh.
>
> —James 3:11-12 (NKJV)

For example, when I decided to get married to my second husband, Neo, I wanted to be honest about my past concerning some of the mistakes I had made. If anything ever came up as our relationship developed, I didn't want him to use that against me. As a result, I told him everything and gave him a chance to back out of marrying me. I wondered if he could accept all of me, the excellent qualities and the questionable ones. I was not emotionally free enough to release all the negative attitudes concerning what I had done, and I continued to punish myself for all my past mistakes and imagined he felt the same way. Once, when we were dating, he said he didn't want to deal with my jealousy, so he wasn't so sure he wanted to keep dating me, but he did.

After three years of dating, I released a barrage of emotions in an outburst, knowing he would no longer want to pursue the relationship. That would have been easier than the usual rejection that had always happened to me once a man found out how disturbed I was. I promised him I had changed, but I would understand if he didn't want me anymore. He still wanted me, and that was a relief.

Neo and I married, he had two children from a previous marriage, I had three and we had two more children together. Life was good, and I finally felt free of all the sin and shame I had created for myself. But Neo was busy in his work and I was involved in mine, not making time for our marriage.

We took for granted that everything was fine until, one day, Cohen walked into my life. This man went out of his way to talk to me and pay me compliments. I thought he was being friendly, but somewhere in the middle of this situation, I found myself wanting to dress up, hoping that Cohen would come into work to see how beautiful I looked. The same pattern that had occurred so many years ago started to repeat itself.

How could this be? I was a godly woman. God had given me a wonderful husband who loved and cherished me, someone who had chosen to marry me after all I had told him. Neo had endured all of the hateful, hurtful words I had said to him because I hated myself. I thought I was changing, so why was I paying so much attention to another man?

He was paying attention to me as well. I learned that Cohen was married, and I asked myself, "Is his infatuation all in my mind?" At first, I pictured him and his wife having such an awesome relationship. Why would he waste his time on me?

All the while, my marriage was gradually slipping away. Neo and I didn't take the time to talk anymore, and it seemed as though he never had time for me. He was always falling asleep when I tried to talk with him. Yet here was Cohen, who wanted to talk. He treated me as if I were exciting. I told myself it wasn't hurting anyone. I noticed that time seemed to stand still when Cohen was around, and no one would come and interrupt us. I knew God had a purpose for this relationship, but what was it? Again, I went searching through the Word seeking answers, looking for permission to justify my actions, and I thought maybe I had made a mistake by getting married and didn't wait long enough for God to bring Cohen into my life.

I looked at all the truths and made up my own. I thought of 2 Corinthians 6:14 (NKJV), "Do not be unequally yoked together with unbelievers." Cohen said that he believed in God—good enough for me! Score one: He is a believer. I twisted and turned this until our relationship looked godly in my eyes.

I didn't hide it. We talked out in the open. I even told Neo that Cohen was my friend, that I didn't want him to interfere with this friendship, and he respected that. He didn't even fight for me, but I wanted him to. I wanted to make him jealous; I wanted him to fight for me and for our marriage. Then one day one of my friends stopped by unexpectedly while we were having a casual conversation and asked us if we were having an affair. Say what? I knew that in my heart I was having an affair, but I would never admit it out loud.

How did I get so blinded by my own sin, and how could I so easily justify this relationship? Sin is sin, I recognized that I had become bitter toward my husband. When I read this Scripture I had a greater understanding of what it meant.

> "No one can serve two masters; for either he will hate the one and love the other, or else he will be loyal to the one and despise the other. You cannot serve God and mammon."
>
> —Matthew 6:24 (NKJV)

Here I was trying to please and serve a man who was not my husband. I started texting Cohen, but I thought I needed more, so I called him. He had given me his number in a business transaction, yet I took it as a secret indication that he wanted me to call him. The first time I called, I felt an uncomfortable shaking of the Holy Spirit convicting me. I sensed the awkwardness of not having anything to say, but that didn't outweigh the need for attention. In my own way, I was saying, "Shut up, Holy Spirit! I got this. You are in my way."

How many times in the past had this happened? Once more, I started creating this ungodly habit of becoming attached to something that wasn't mine. I was hoping somewhere in the back in my mind that Cohen would abandon his wife and his present situation and choose me. I believed he wanted to leave her as much as I wanted him to. I convinced myself all the signs were there showing that God wanted me with Cohen.

Soon, I began to despise my husband. He didn't understand me. He didn't do anything the way I thought he should, and I grew resentful toward him. I asked myself if I could leave this life. We now had seven children. What would they think of me? Where was God? I told God I trusted Him. Did I really? To whom was I listening?

I was convinced my way was better, but when I really looked at it compared to what God says, my way was full of secrets. I hurt others, and people were getting mad at me. I justified my behavior again, however. Cohen was like the father I'd never had. This picture was one way I tried to justify this new relationship with the lies I believed.

Again, Satan never makes sin look evil or hurtful. He makes it appear appealing and beautiful, and, like Eve, once I took the bite my eyes were opened, and I could see clearly. I was becoming paranoid and defensive, making excuses, and starting to hide.

Even so, I found out that God was there from the very start. He said, "Over here, Michelle. Here is your way of escape. Come to me, and I will give you rest. I will fill you up." Unfortunately, once more I chose to follow my own selfish desires. How could I have spit in His face?

I became angry at myself for getting seduced right back in the same trap I'd been in before. I knew better. How did this happen again? Cohen and I made a decision to stop talking and end this friendship. As soon as I agreed, the fear and guilt washed over me, even though we made a mutual agreement it felt abrupt, a habit I had formed to fill my need for value that just dropped out of my life. That wasn't fair. How many times had I had a friend dump me for no apparent reason? This felt the same way.

Up until then, whenever I had started to feel unloved, insecure, and unattractive, I'd reached out to Cohen to feel fulfilled. I noticed that what had filled me up ran out rather quickly. It hurt, but I had created this bad habit. How was I going to get out of it? In the same way I'd entered the relationship: one uncomfortable step at a time.

I began to examine this bad habit and ask why I sought out a toxic relationship again. I thought about my marriage and how I had made a commitment to my husband to love and cherish him no matter what. I then thought about how God loves me no matter what I do or how I treat Him. Neo, the man whom God put into my life all those years ago, was still there, and I used to think he was everything great. What changed? God doesn't throw me away when I'm not lovable. He waits patiently for me to draw near to Him.

I also thought about the tables being turned and wondered how I would feel if Neo were doing what I was doing. It didn't feel very good. I had made a promise, a commitment. I had a covenant agreement with my husband. Was I serious about it? Was God serious about having a covenant relationship with me? His promises are true. He never lies, but here I was claiming to be a Christian and loving God and living my life lying and cheating, coveting, and so much more. When was I going to decide to let go and trust God as I had said I did many years before?

I decided to trust God with all of my emptiness and ask Him to fill me. Every time I felt alone, depressed, empty, and unloved, I reached for my Bible. I read and talked to God. I began journaling. He filled me, and He restored my soul (Psalms 23:3). He showed me where I had been selfish and uncommitted.

Where was God? He was always there waiting with His arms wide open, waiting for me to run to Him. I have pictured God longing for my love and seeing me running toward Him only to jet past Him to someone else and seeing the grieving look on His face as I chose a man over Him. Despite that, He still waits, waits for me to choose Him. He is a true gentleman, waiting for us to choose, waiting for us to run into His arms to let Him love on us and heal all the wounds we have inflicted on ourselves or someone has inflicted on us.

I thought I knew what was better for me. God told me what was best for me, but I did not believe. I did not trust that He knew what He was talking about. I sought my need for love and acceptance my way, but it did not fill my need. God is the only one who knows how to fill us and knows exactly what we need and when we need it. Only He can do that.

Marriage is like a garden we have to tend. It needs love, care, water, fertilizer, and we must pull the weeds—all of this takes time. When we neglect to tend our garden, the weeds begin to choke the growing plants, and intruders may come. They could be our friends or our work. When we make time for God and our marriage, there is no room for intruders to come. Although they attempt to enter the garden that has been nurtured and cared for, intruders are unsuccessful because the garden continues to thrive in a fulfilling environment and has solid boundaries.

Our relationship with Jesus is the same way. We need to find a time during the day that allows us to spend time with Him where we take time to read the Word, seek His advice, and listen when He tells us the elements we need to weed from our lives. We can show His love by going out of our way to be especially loving to our spouse, to go above and beyond what others expect.

As we walk in the Spirit and strive to be more like Jesus, we must ask the Holy Spirit to reveal areas in our lives where we need to remove weeds. Here are examples of some of those bad habits:

- Interrupting people or not allowing them to finish what they are saying
- Not listening
- Entertaining negative thoughts instead of replacing them when they first come to mind.
- Poor time management
- Taking out frustrations on our spouse or trying to make them our spouse's problem
- Trying to solve others' problems and not our own

We also need to take the time to be with our spouse and listen to what they are saying, find out their love language, and fill their cup. For many years, I was trying to fill Neo's cup with my love language, until one day I wondered why the principles of the book didn't seem to be working. In the book *The Five Love Languages*, Gary Chapman outlines five different ways that people understand and perceive love: words of affirmation, quality time, receiving gifts, acts of service, and physical touch.

I thought if I loved Neo with my love language, he would know how to love me. I tried to lead by example, but it didn't work. I learned we get the privilege of loving our spouses with *their* love language. For example, Neo's love language is "words of affirmation." Mine is "quality time." If I'm not giving him words of affirmation, then he doesn't feel like giving me quality time and vice versa.

Recognizing Temptation

When we notice we are being tempted, we get to decide whether we are going to draw near to Jesus or whether we want to move away from Him so that we don't feel convicted. Of course, we will feel a strong conviction at first, but the more we ignore it, the more we become immune to it and soon don't notice it at all. Our feelings turn from conviction to justification. As stated previously, Satan doesn't present sin as hideous and unattractive; on the contrary, what he offers is appealing to our senses. He knows our weaknesses and knows how to make sin enticing. For this reason, most importantly, we must develop a close relationship with God and stay in the Word. As we study the Word through His message He will expose the natural and spiritual motivations of a believer's heart.

> For the word of God *is* living and powerful, and sharper than any two-edged sword, piercing even to division of soul and spirit, and of joints and

marrow, and is a discerner of the thoughts and intents of the heart.

—Hebrews 4:12 (NKJV)

When we accept Jesus as our personal savior His Spirit then dwells with in us, the Holy Spirit, who guides and directs us and teaches us all truth, and brings to remembrance all things that He has said. John 14:26(NKJV)

A good example of how the Holy Spirit directed me in my life would be when I talked myself into having an affair. I created a dishonest motive and I deceived myself into thinking that I had a right and deserved something different. As I read the Word, God showed me what His truth was. God said I should not covet what belongs to someone else. To covet someone else's spouse and to think the grass is greener at the neighbor's house is coveting! I asked Him to help me re-process my thinking and behavior. I honestly believed I deserved to have what I wanted There was no peace in what I was doing. I now like to ask, "What is my motive?" before I'm about to do something. What is the real reason I want to do whatever I am about to do or talk to a certain person about something? I am continually analyzing my motive in situations where I act or speak and express my views. Often, I ask God to show me if I am being honest with myself, and is what I am wanting to do in line with His ways.

Every time we choose to sin, we open a door for Satan to set up spiritual strongholds in our lives. It's similar to inviting him to our party and giving him permission to enter. A stronghold is a behavior individuals hold onto that ends up holding onto them. Such conduct owns you, and you can't handle it. The sin we commit to open the door to create a stronghold in our life will cause us as much pain, if not more, to get rid of them. In the end, after we push through the suffering and pain, our lives will be so much brighter, and we will experience more freedom than we ever had before.

Many times when I felt insecure and needed love and acceptance and someone of the opposite sex complimented me, my mind would jump to attention, and I'd feel a connection or start to fantasize. In that moment, I had the choice either to accept the compliment or to go about my day feeling good about the positive feedback and our conversation. Many times, I would entertain the thought that maybe that person was making advances toward me or there was some ulterior motive attached to it. As such situations occurred, I learned that my individual responsibility was to stop that temptation before it grew into sin.

Temptation is not a sin, but what we do with the temptation can lead to sin. We can cast it out or entertain it. If we spend any time entertaining it, it becomes sin. As soon as we notice ourselves entertaining anything that does not produce the fruit of the Spirit, we must stop, repent (change our mind), and get back to healthy thinking.

Renewing Our Mind

Renewing our minds involves changing the negative meaning we have attached to a previous adverse experience and giving it a positive meaning. If we constantly tell ourselves we do not measure up to the expectations of others, we must stop and remember that God has forgiven us. He loves us, we are His children. We can turn any negative thinking we have into a positive statement and speak the positive words to ourselves. We can also speak God's promises out loud so our ears can hear them. We listen to our own voice all the time, so let's love our own selves so we can love others. Remember: Love your neighbor as yourself.

Another way we can renew our mind is through gratitude. If nothing seems to be going our way, and we are feeling less confident, we ought to start thanking God for everything we see and everyone in our lives. When our view toward ourselves begins to shift, we can feel hopeful and see the light shining before us. We ought to thank Him even for all the blessings we've encountered along the way and all the heartache as well. Where would we be today had we not gone through those situations? We are the persons we are today because of the trials and tests we have gone through triumphantly.

> Consider it pure joy, my brothers, whenever you face trials of many kinds, because you know the

testing of your faith develops perseverance, perseverance must finish its work so that you may be mature and complete not lacking anything.

—James 1:2–4 (NIV)

Another great way to renew your mind is to memorize a verse that speaks to you in the area where you are struggling. Sometimes I will say a verse several times until I feel a shift in my thinking. I suggest giving it a try. If we struggle with getting rid of the temptation, we get to make the choice to confess it to God and ask Him to help us, and He will. He already knows our struggle with whatever we are going through; He is waiting for us to ask for help.

"So I say to you, ask, and it will be given to you; seek, and you will find; knock, and it will be opened to you. For everyone who asks receives, and he who seeks finds, and to him who knocks it will be opened."

—Luke 11:9, 10 (NKJV)

I have learned that anger is a bad habit, and only by the grace of God and His Word of light can we overcome any sin. God is not limited or confined by our mistakes.
But He gives more grace. Therefore He says:

"God resists the proud, But gives grace to the humble."

> Therefore submit to God. Resist the devil, and he will flee from you.
> Draw near to God and He will draw near to you.
>
> —James 4:6-8a (NKJV)

Tell God where your mind is straying, ask for forgiveness, and ask Him to help you overcome your fleshly desire. I let go of my pent-up anger by asking God to forgive me. Then I forgave myself and I asked Him to change my thinking. It was then I let go of Anger.

CHAPTER 7

Transparency Brings Healing

As believers, we must become transparent before God and expose the negative, the positive, the lustful, and the ugly thoughts we are having. He already knows what we have been thinking, but when we bring our thoughts into His light, He can help us overcome any challenge. He will even help us change our minds. We can tell him exactly what we have been scheming, pondering, and planning to create without Him. We get to ask Him to reveal His truth to us and to open our hearts and minds to receive what He teaches us. God, our heavenly Father, is the wisest of all parents. He knows when our desires will jeopardize our character or if they will glorify Him.

Our spirit is the Holy Spirit who resides in us; our soul is the carnal part of ourselves. When our words and actions don't line up with the Word of God, we find conflict within. Turmoil in our soul shows that our spirit knows what we want and need, yet our soul seems to contradict that need. Our spirit and soul need to work together or we become discontented. Regarding the conflict between the Spirit and the flesh, the one we consistently feed will always win.

> What causes fight and quarrels among you? Don't they come from your desires that battle within you? You want something but don't get it.
> You kill and covet, but you cannot have what you want. You quarrel and fight.
> You do not have, because you do not ask God. When you ask, you do not receive, because you ask with the wrong motives, that you may spend what you get on your pleasures.
>
> —James 4:1–3 (NIV)

Confessing our sinful behavior offers us an opportunity to probe deeply into our souls to examine our motives, allowing us a chance to repent for our actions. For example, perhaps we responded to something sinfully because it made us feel loved or because we were lashing out at someone. They had hurt us, so we retaliated. But our responsibility was not to pay back.

Transparency Brings Healing

"*Vengeance is Mine, I will repay,*" says the Lord.

—Romans 12:19b (NKJV).

The Book of Proverbs advises us to heap hot coals on our enemies' heads by doing good to them. This is similar to the fiery love of Jesus, according to Joyce Meyer.[8] You are probably familiar with the sayings "kill them with kindness" and "if you can't say something nice, say nothing at all" (see Deuteronomy 32:35, Proverbs 25:22, Romans 12:22, Matthew 5:43, 44). That advice especially applies to believers.

I think about all of the years I have wasted being angry, about the many relationships I have thrown away because I was angry with myself for not listening to my heavenly Father who knows all and knows best. When I please men instead of God, I come up short every time, which causes grief and anger all over again. I beat myself up and call myself stupid for not getting it one more time. I have learned to set boundaries for myself and to do what's best for me and to seek God as I walk forward.

When we knowingly behave in a harmful way or pursue unrighteous goals, we are only thinking about our selfish desire for satisfaction. Only after that do we start to be concerned about what someone else thinks.

As we seek to please man, we ought to ask ourselves, "What is my motive? Why do I care what this person thinks?" In my case, I wanted respect. I had asked Cohen if he respected me. Of course, he told me he did. Yet as the relationship escalated, I lost respect for both him and myself.

I understood why I kept going back, seeking one man after another for that conversation, for that phone call. When I was experiencing low self-esteem, I needed someone to show love and acceptance and to tell me that I was terrific, beautiful, and perfect, and that I had a great smile. I would then start to justify why I initiated the conversation by remembering what I'd heard other people say:

> *If it feels good, do it.*
> *You only live once.*
> *You don't know if you will even be alive tomorrow, so live in the moment.*
> *You deserve it.*
> *You didn't ask for this.*
> *There is a reason God put this person in your life.*

Yes, the reason was so I could die to my carnal desires and to seek God's face. Then I could believe that He wants what is good for me! I have come to know that the prize for turning from temptation is more rewarding as I experience love for myself. The outcome of turning from the temptation helps me stay focused on who God says I am in the Word. This victory brings with it more love, fulfillment, and acceptance with lasting results far beyond a moment of self-motivated satisfaction.

Transparency Brings Healing

It's easy to fall back into our bad habits because we are familiar with the techniques we created to self-protect and provide for ourselves, and we think we are prospering from our schemes. Because we already know the outcome, we also know our satisfaction is only temporary, but we are hoping this time it will be for real. Only the Lord Jesus Christ, whose promises are true, is truly satisfying. I cannot say that enough.

When the Holy Spirit tells us to move forward or to refrain from acting, we always have a choice. We can proceed with our initial impulse and move ahead, or we can heed His warning and run in the other direction. He always supplies all we need. The Spirit will make the way clear, for He has gone before us. We must seek Him and die to our own evil desires.

We have a choice: We can follow what our flesh or human nature wants (what we know and think we are in control of, which always gets us into trouble), or we can follow the Holy Spirit's lead, by aligning our words and actions with the Word of God, as our spirit and soul work together we will experience results in love in the lives of everyone involved. This results in a win-win for all.

We can learn so much from Adam and Eve and what happened as soon as they took that bite of fruit. It's exactly what happened when I first decided to play around with temptation just a little. I became self-conscious and aware of betrayal, anger, rage, regret, blame, failed expectations, bitterness, low self-worth, insecurity, guilt, and shame. My eyes were opened at once, and I couldn't go back.

So, now what?

When I look at all the mistakes I've made, I am grateful that I can be free from all my transgressions as long as I ask for forgiveness. God has given us these beautiful gifts of reconciliation and forgiveness, so why are we hesitant to use them?

The verb form of reconciliation is to reconcile, to settle or resolve, to bring (oneself) to accept.[9]

Jesus wants us to come to Him, repent, and forgive ourselves. We need to let the old man die. When we don't, we create a means for Satan to come against us. Satan loves to initiate self-hatred, guilt, shame, blame, and isolation so he can whisper in our ear what horrible people we are. We then begin to think everyone knows, and we judge ourselves more harshly. We begin to think we are not worthy of anyone's love, feeling unattractive and hopeless or feeling we have destroyed ourselves. Then we start blaming all the other circumstances in our lives. We even start believing God doesn't want anything to do with us because we have become so corrupt. So we begin punishing ourselves. Gradually, we expect no forgiveness for ourselves or for anyone else; such thinking leads to explosive rage and anger that anything can trigger.

For these reasons, we are to put our trust in Jesus, as we lay aside all our burdens, all our fears, all our foolish behaviors at His feet. We can ask God to "Create in me a clean heart" as Psalms 51:10 states if we ask Him to, He will change our hearts and fill us. The lyrics to this song make a similar request:

> Change my heart oh God,
> Make it ever true
> Change my heart oh God
> May I be like You
>
> Eddie Espinosa[10]

He already knows when we are going to miss the mark before we do. Since He has gone before us, He knows when we are going to choose our flesh over His spirit. For example, when I thought I finally had my life all together, temptation came again. It was the same as before but just looked different. I thought I was strong and wouldn't fall into sin again. I asked, "Why do I behave the way I don't want to?" I was transparent with God. I sought after Him, I told Him how I felt about everything that was going on. He reminded me that we are children of the highest King. He has our back and watches over us. We only need to rest in Him, meaning we don't need to worry or feel confused about anything. We must have faith and believe that, no matter what, God watches out for us, and we have peace. Finally, we are not to worry or become anxious about anything.

When we seek Him every moment of every day, He will rescue us in those moments of distrust and doubt. Our first response in any situation must be to trust God and not to worry. We must speak out and say, "I trust you God." In Philippians 4:6–7 He says that we are to be anxious for nothing, but in everything by prayer and supplication, with thanksgiving, to let your requests be made known to God. As we ask, seek, and knock, the peace of God, which surpasses all understanding will guard our hearts and minds through Christ Jesus.

We must look away from anything that distracts us from Jesus, the author and finisher of our faith. We get to choose to look to God, think about Him, speak of His goodness, focus on faith, and as we use our faith, we will find that it grows. The more we use it, the more familiar we become with it. If we are worrying or fretting over any circumstance, and if we do not have peace flowing through our body, we know we are not trusting God. As soon as we start reasoning and trying to figure out how to solve the problem and stressing over whatever we are doing, we are taking it out of God's hands. Peace, be still. We could say a prayer like this:

Dear Lord, I am fearfully and wonderfully made. Forgive me, Lord, for not trusting You. I give You this worry, this worry about how relationships and everyday life will turn out. I thank You for showing me how to trust You in any and every situation I encounter. Lord, You are my strength and my song; You are my joy and my peace. Praise You, Lord Jesus. Forgive me for worrying, for You will not give me more than I can bear. Thank you, Lord. Amen.

Prayer is a powerful tool against worry. As soon as we enter into prayer and thanksgiving, our world changes around us. We can repeat "I trust you, God" over and over until our mood changes and shifts into a positive, peaceful mode. Again, the more we practice the easier it becomes.

When we accepted Jesus as our Lord and Savior, we received salvation, along with the fruit of the Spirit. Now we say, "What do I do with all these amazing gifts?" We start and continue practicing and operating them. Developing a beautiful relationship with Jesus takes spending time with Him in His Word. It takes practicing love, joy, peace, long-suffering, kindness, goodness, faithfulness, gentleness, and self-control: the fruit of the Spirit He gave to us (Galatians 5:22, 23). This practice involves falling short, asking Him what we need to know, having an open heart and mind to listen to what He has to say, and then repenting or changing our mind and behaving differently.

We can develop all the fruit of the Spirit in the same way we develop our bodies when we exercise our muscles to get stronger. If we have a bad habit of opening our mouths without thinking, we can ask God, "What do You want me to know right now?" If you don't hear an answer, ask Him whom you need to forgive. We could possibly want to control the situation, get our own way, or gain something for ourselves.

Practicing self-control will help us have more self-respect. When we face any decisions—whether great or insignificant, easy or difficult—we have opportunities to practice self-control and wait until we have a clear answer before taking a step that we may regret. We are to be led by peace, not excitement. We tell ourselves, "I am content and emotionally stable."

We must remember God's voice stills us, comforts, encourages, calms, convicts, leads, assures, and enlightens us. In contrast, Satan's voice rushes, pushes, frightens, confuses, discourages, worries, and condemns, according to an unknown author[11]. This is a good indicator of whose voice you are listening to.

God owns everything and knows every need we have, when we are craving man's approval or attention. If we will run into Jesus's arms, and ask His advice. If we are loving Him with all our heart, mind, soul, and strength, we will be satisfied with the answer He gives us and trust He knows exactly what He is doing. The more we trust the answers He gives and the more we practice our faith, the stronger our faith will become. We will also recognize the lies of the enemy more quickly.

Satan tempts us with situations that seem spontaneous and full of pleasure while having little responsibility. Joyce Meyer reminds us[12], "You cannot be what Christ wants you to be if you are hanging out eating at the buffet of the enemy or indulging in things that make you feel good at the time."[13] They wear off or end with a bad taste in our mouth. God's way never ends; we keep reaching new heights of fulfillment. There is no greater high than Jesus Christ. He is exciting, exhilarating, and mysterious with a great sense of humor. He always knows what we need precisely when we need it. He is truly amazing.

God Makes All Things New

> "Behold, I make all things new," And He said to me, "Write, for these words are true and faithful." And He said to me, "It is done! I am the Alpha and the Omega, the Beginning and the End. I will give of the fountain of the water of life freely to him who thirsts. He who overcomes shall inherit all things, and I will be his God and he shall be My son.
>
> —Revelation 21:5b–7 (NKJV)

To overcome evil with good, all one has to do is spend time with Jesus and develop a relationship with Him in the same way we would put energy into any other relationship. He is the best friend to have. Here are a few steps to begin the practice of getting to know Him.

1. Each day set aside some time to read your Bible, to record your thoughts in a journal, and to pray. I first started to journal when I began complaining to my supervisor about a co-worker with aggravating behavior. One day my supervisor handed me a journal, and from that day forward I began to put some of my thoughts on paper. In the beginning I wrote down a few verses that really spoke to me. I'd spend about five minutes writing, and five minutes grew to ten and to even more time until it soon seemed like there was no time for anything else. I started to write about some of my frustrations, and I asked God questions. After venting to God in my journal, I began to read my Bible. That's when I would find my answer or He would show me a Scripture that pertained to the complaint I was having. I would get to think about it all day, and the healing began.

2. It is important to ask God to speak to you through His Word before you begin to read. When I started praying that prayer, I began to understand His Word more clearly.

3. Before you start to go about your day, ask God to bring to remembrance all that He taught you in

your quiet time. I find that if a question comes up during the day, the answer is always exactly what I studied in the Bible that morning or a previous morning. God has already gone before me and knows exactly what I am going to need.

As we do this, amazingly, a shift will take place in our lives. Sometimes things may become worse, but as we press through each situation, and draw closer to God and the devil will flee. As we spend more time with Him, we will find we long to be with Him more and more. We talk to Him all day, for He is always with us. He has sent His Holy Spirit to guide us into all truths.

Life can be devastating if we let our lives unfold as they always have. When we stumble or fall, we must stop and ask God where we went astray, and we must repent. We then ask Him what He wants us to do and proceed to do it. If we need to get in a quiet spot, there is always the stall in the restroom. However, with Jesus Christ and the Holy Spirit to guide us into all truths, we can more readily follow the will of God and all His truths begin to align. Our transparency with Him opens the door for the healing to begin.

CHAPTER 8

Looking Beyond Self

Because of the paths I chose to follow, I caused a chain reaction, either positive or negative. I thought everyone was conspiring and retaliating against me. In reality, I was hindering my own progress by judging myself and using others to take the attention away from me and blaming them for my misery. The judgment came back to me in the same measure by which I judged others. I had to change my thinking, renew my mind, and then my world started to turn around for me.

When someone walks past you and doesn't speak to you, do you get offended? If we stop and think about it, perhaps we'd realize they were having a bad day.

Perhaps they were in deep thought about something else. Perhaps something was troubling them. Instead of getting offended, we ought to tell ourselves "it's not about me" and then pray for the people involved. It will release us from the old comfortable routine of thinking negative thoughts.

> "Judge not, that you be not judged. For with what judgment you judge, you will be judged; and with the measure you use, it will be measured back to you."
>
> —Matthew 7:1, 2(NKJV)

When I was feeling insecure and acting as if everyone were against me, I told myself, "It is not about me," and this has been helpful. I have even written the words on my hand to remind me. It has been a powerful tool to help me let go of that negative thinking.

What I thought others were thinking about me was actually what I thought about myself. For example, I cheated on my husband Barrett and found myself searching for love and acceptance anywhere I could get them. I thought he felt the same way, so I would accuse him of doing or thinking the same way I did.

In another situation, when I was giving someone a piece of my mind, I noticed the words coming out of my mouth were expressing how I felt, as if I had been speaking directly to myself instead of the person to whom I was directing my words. Sometimes the situation seemed similar to an out-of-body experience, as if I've been lifted out of my own body and was watching from above. When I screamed out my frustration, that was how I felt about something I hadn't accomplished but wanted others to do for me. I made it their fault. If it's *their* fault, then I don't have to look at it anymore because I shifted the responsibility to them.

When the tables are turned and the person we are speaking with becomes frustrated with us, we can take a different perspective when they express views that differ from ours. Instead of getting offended, we ought to listen as if what they are saying is them telling us how they feel about themselves. Of course we get to examine ourselves first and make sure we haven't offended them. When we practice doing this instead of taking on everyone else's garbage, we will be free of being offended because "It's not about you."

Forgiving yourself

I've overcome the anger and have forgiven myself and anyone else I need to forgive. When I am not sure if there is someone else I need to forgive, I ask the Holy Spirit, "Is there anyone else I need to forgive?" If I refuse to forgive, I block the flow of the Holy Spirit. He is so gracious that He will tell us everything we need to know. We merely have to ask, and we receive what we ask.

Why should I forgive them when they are guilty? I thought of the verse Colossians 3:13 *"even as Christ forgave you, so you must do."* When I see myself from their perspective, as if I am the one who wronged them, would I not want them to forgive me? Indeed, I would want them to be forgiving and give me another chance to correct the situation. God offers countless opportunities to do the right thing, so that I will do the same for others.

One day when I had gone to town with my husband Neo, we were fighting, and I was furious with him, so angry I could not stay in his presence. We entered the business where we had a meeting, and I refused to change my hostile attitude, so I marched out across the parking lot crying to wait in the truck where I could vent to God. I took out my journal and began to write. "Lord, why is he like this and why do you expect me always to forgive him when he keeps acting out in the same way?"

I then heard the Holy Spirit say, "I forgive you over and over again" Ouch! He was right. I thought of all the times I'd misbehaved and asked for forgiveness, not just from God but from other people as well. I wanted them to know how sorry I was and so desired their forgiveness. I also realized how one-sided I had been most of my life. I wanted people to forgive me, but I wanted to hold a grudge and make them pay. At that moment, I decided I would change my attitude about forgiving.

> For as he thinks in his heart, so *is* he.
>
> —Proverbs 23:7(NKJV)

The energy we put forth comes back to us. We can test the theory this way: Have you ever noticed when you are in a bad mood at church or work and you have been having negative thoughts all day that nobody comes around to talk to you? You are putting off negative energy. The field around you radiates negative vibes as if to say, "Stay away from me!" You naturally repel others with your negative energy.

On the other hand, when you have a positive attitude, have wholesome thoughts, and have the joy of the Lord radiating from within, you attract people to your presence by the sweet-smelling fragrance of the Holy Spirit. It's as if people are lining up to talk to you. It's a fun-filled experiment that shows the power of the love of Jesus.

Abundant Living

James Richards states we attract the same qualities to us because we imprint them on our heart based on what we believe. If we believe the promises of God, we will have an abundant life. What is abundant life? I believe we see abundant life when a problem arises or when we are not feeling secure and we choose to seek our Heavenly Father and our friendship with Him. Through the Word,

God instructs us to examine the truth that will direct us through any trial or problem we face.

Instead of putting ourselves directly in the middle of the problem or trial, we ought to set it on the table and look at it as if it's not really our dilemma. We examine other people's problems or trials, seeking a solution to their problem, yet when it's our own, these issues seem different and more difficult to solve. However, the Scripture says, "do not worry;"

> "Therefore I say to you, do not worry about your life, what you will eat or what you will drink; nor about your body, what you will put on. Is not life more than food and the body more than clothing? But seek first the kingdom of God and His righteousness, and all these things shall be added unto you. Therefore do not worry about tomorrow, for tomorrow will worry about its own things. Sufficient for the day is its own trouble."
>
> —Matthew 6: 25, 33-34 (NKJV)

When we genuinely apply this way of thinking, we are living an abundant life, trusting that we don't have to worry about anything. We are confident a chair will hold us as soon as we sit down; we never doubt that the chair is going to support us before we take a seat. When we put that kind of faith into every relationship, problem, sickness, and worry, we are living an abundant life.

Listening to the Holy Spirit

When we tell God how we feel and listen to Him and follow His direction. We must not seek other people's opinions to please them, and we must not base our actions on what they think is good for us. We get to search our own heart for what we want, or more importantly, what God wants for our lives. If we listen to the advice of man instead of God, we will reap what we sow, so let's sow beautiful words and actions to glorify God and seek His approval. We must make up our mind ahead of time that when adverse circumstances come, we will recognize them for what they really are: lies from the enemy. The enemy is not always Satan; our flesh is our enemy as well. "You can even justify these behaviors and dress them up to appear spiritual," says Joyce Meyer.[14]

Just as He promises, the Holy Spirit always warns us before we step into danger. It's up to us to have our ears and eyes open. Similar to Psalm 119:18 we ask, "Lord give me eyes to see and ears to hear."

How do we know when the Holy Spirit is talking to us? I like to think of it as "first thought, best thought," and anything after that tries to talk us into something or reason with us to talk us out of something. There are no guarantees, but we get to act on our faith believing that the first answer that comes to mind is from the Holy Spirit. Most of the time the best answer or decision doesn't make sense to our logical mind. Having a relationship with Jesus is all about trusting that He is going to lead us in the right direction.

When I have a decision to make and I'm not sure what to do, the peace of God comes when I am moving in the direction He wants me to move. I have personally gone with my first thought by faith and believed it was, indeed, the way to go. It was that stirring inside, thinking "What if it is the right answer?" and going with it. We must be willing to accept what God is giving to us or we won't receive it. Everything depends on our willingness to receive what God has freely given us. He is a gentleman and never forces Himself on anyone. He wants us to love Him so much that He desires that we come to Him out of love, not out of duty.

I like to picture myself as a little child when I am hurting or in need of advice, comfort, love, or acceptance. I can run to my Father God, jump in His lap, and tell Him what has happened or sob in relief on His chest. I picture Him holding me and telling me it's going to be all right. He reminds me of so many promises and truths that make me feel better. He also shows me and whispers in His still small voice how much He adores and delights in me. I want to please Him, and I love doing what He asks and being what He has created me to be. It's like doing something special for the one you love. Loving God is just like that, only He never disappoints me. He is always gentle and never makes me feel blame, shame, or guilt.

Nearly every human being I have ever put my trust in has let me down in one way or another. I look back over my life and see all the times God was there for me. I also see all the times I didn't listen to Him and received the consequences of my actions because I was trying to be my own protector and provider.

Every time I asked God for direction, He always answered me. Many times I was unwilling to receive His guidance, and as a result, I encountered much heartache. He gave me good advice to keep my heart safe because He is such a good Father. Recognizing that I had rejected God's instruction for my life was hard, knowing that I could have prevented all of that heartache and turmoil in my life. I continued to choose this path over and over again because I thought I knew best. Pride entered into the situation. Sin looked more enticing than loving God.

The world says God is boring and that we have to be free from sin and live a holy and righteous life or He will strike us with a lightning bolt. As far as I can remember, I always believed this. I didn't know how to love myself, let alone God. I thought He was keeping pleasures from me that I liked or that I thought would make me happy. I set out to prove that I could direct my life, but all I ever confirmed was that when I try to control my own life, all I get is rejection, pain, and heartache.

When I finally surrendered my life to Him and listened to everything He said, I found that I could have more abundant joy, peace, patience, and love. I've also learned that I can trust Him and that He does take care of me. My only job is to believe Him and have faith that He will do what He says. I have experienced His guidance time and time again. I encourage anyone who wants more love to trust Him because He is where real life begins and ends. He is by far the opposite of boring. He offers eternal life with no beginning or end. It is constant if we choose to enter into His grace and mercy.

CHAPTER 9

Guarding Our Hearts From Hurt

In the past when someone has hurt me or when I thought someone had offended me, I wanted to show them how it felt by retaliating in return. Over the years, I have noticed my behavior, and I have wondered about the words I spoke or how I responded to painful situations. I have asked if feeling rejection, abandonment, or some other negative emotion caused me to anticipate that all of my relationships would turn sour. Whenever I say something like this is going to happen, it always does. As I look back to speaking negative pronouncements out loud was similar to a magician waving his wand, in that my words had creative power, either positively or negatively.

I expected others to reject me, and so it happened just as I thought. Why? Because I created it. I created the negative circumstances in my mind before they happened. The negative words I spoke created what I feared would happen. My subconscious heard the words of my mouth and said "okay" and went to work to bring to pass what I just said. This process also works the same way with the positive words we speak.

Because of my past wounds, I created a pattern to self-protect. Here is an example: One night Neo and I went to a banquet. We were approached by a man who proceeded to tell the story of another woman bringing Neo lunch when he was at work. The *fear* in me started to peak, and I rehearsed a series of scenes in my head. I thought this woman must be prettier, smarter, and something more than I ever was, and I started feeling as if I was *not enough*. The temptation to verbally rip my husband's head right off came to the forefront. I felt betrayed. I then had a decision to make: Was I going to *sin* and show everyone how insecure I was by letting him have it in front of everyone, or was I going to keep my composure since I had already decided he was *guilty*?

This type of situation happened to me all through my high school years and during my first marriage. As a result, I thought I ought to be used to the enemy's schemes by now. I wondered how I always got blindsided by situations like this.

I was overly concerned about what other people would think if I lashed out in public. I thought I could keep my composure until I reached the car, and then I was going to let him have it with both barrels. I was already thinking about divorce. I became so upset that we had to leave the banquet before it even started, and when we left, my husband was at the end of a barrage of foul words as all my pain came out. I tried to hurt him from every conceivable direction. As it turned out, he was innocent, and the incident related to another man with the same name. The guy telling the story was mad at my husband and was trying to get back at him.

We must learn that when we have negative thoughts, we ought to look at them and create positive outcomes to counteract the negative with a positive. We can look at what has gone wrong in the past and decide to do something different this time. We must be deliberate, and it may take a few times to identify our bad habits of speaking or behaving inappropriately, but the effort we put forth will be worth our time and effort to improve. When we ask God, He will reveal the areas where we need to change. For this approach to work, we must sincerely seek a different outcome. Otherwise, we will continue to see the same results because our habits are still the same. There will be no change until we change what we say and do.

If everyone applied the golden rule and treated others how they would like to be treated, there would be less fighting and fewer heartaches. We need to learn that when someone behaves in an inappropriate way, their action may affect us, but their decisions have nothing to do with our reaction. We get to choose how we respond to the situation.

Occasionally, if my spouse hurt my feelings or I thought he misunderstood me or I sadly sensed he wasn't listening to me, I wanted to show him how it felt. To do this, I kept certain information from him instead of communicating my needs responsibly. When I examined my motives as to why I was withholding information from him, I discovered my true motives. I was actually being vindictive, but I didn't want to consider that. I called it showing him the truth, my truth. I felt gratified promoting this vengeful attitude because I thought he deserved to be hurt because of something he had done or had failed to do for me, so I'd "show him"!

I would justify my thoughts and actions by blaming my spouse for not paying attention to me, for failing to compliment me, or because he was never home. Many times I felt like he was unfaithful, so I had a right to retaliate, to show him how it felt. I started doubting the reasons we married in the first place. The accusations and responses continued, and before I knew it, I was out of control. Truthfully, I was not hurting my spouse, but I was hurting myself. I was being selfish by not talking to my husband and telling him how I felt, and to pray and trust God to make all things new.

I would ask God to show me the weeds that I needed to remove from my life. When He revealed one of the weeds was my seeking a man who was not my husband, I didn't want to let him go because I had made him my god. I would get my confidence through him. This is one way of guarding my heart, or self-protecting. If I were bored or feeling unfulfilled, I'd go to him for a quick fix of reassurance. If he wasn't available, I became angry because I didn't get my way or irritated because his wife needed him. What about me? Really?

Creating such a bad habit and putting someone else in place of God is very frustrating. We ask what is keeping us from obeying God—it's fear. Fear that He won't provide us with something better, and then we will be alone. Fear of removing the person we have placed in our life to make us happy. We must recognize no individual can ever fulfil us; even our spouse will eventually disappoint us.

When we have a strong relationship with the Lord Jesus Christ, He will get us through anything. Love is a choice, not a feeling. When we go back to the covenant agreement we made on our wedding day, we must remember it was a choice. Think about how our spouse would feel if they knew we were keeping secrets. How would we feel if our spouse were doing what we are doing? If we are doing something that will hurt our marriage in any way, we need to ask God to help us change our mind.

Repentance

We must confess to God, our Father, and tell Him how we are feeling when we are desiring this other person who is not our spouse. Ask God to fill us up, to fill that void. We may even need to confess to Him that we don't want Him to change our mind. He even knows that about us, and He wants us to ask Him to help us. Once we confess every evil thought, then He can work a miracle in us.

We must remember we will go through a period of time mourning over our idol, but we should earnestly seek God and continually submit our challenging situations to Him. If we do this, we will be free. Our chains will have been broken. Praise the Lord. When we are feeling lonely, we need only seek God, and He will be there. When we are feeling empty or depressed, feeling inadequate and unattractive, we seek God, and He will fill us up with whatever we need.

God has promised He will never leave us nor forsake us. He is always available to uplift us whenever and wherever we need Him. He is the same yesterday, today, and forever. He is trustworthy and never lies, cheats, or steals. He is beautiful. God's kindness leads us to repentance. It's His tender hand tapping us on the shoulder—sometimes yanking us by the collar to save us from destruction—as He leads us back to His life-giving side. To experience the full life Jesus longs to give, we must begin with repentance.

We can follow the path based on our feelings, or we can follow the path that we know is the right way to go. To make the right choice means we discipline ourselves to behave in a way that we don't feel like behaving, but we know it is the right way to conduct our lives. Making the right decision is dying to self. Discipline doesn't bring immediate joy, but later it does bring lasting joy.

The enemy is always out to destroy us, and he often tries to influence us to make poor choices—to choose to do what feels good or is easy at the moment instead of what will be beneficial in the long run. These choices may temporarily satisfy the flesh (self), but they don't please God, nor do they produce fulfillment. We ought to discipline ourselves to make wise choices that honor God and His Word.

God encourages His children to walk in the Spirit, and we do that by choosing to do what is right, even if it doesn't seem to feel good, at the time. We don't want to let our mind wander and do whatever it pleases, for we become whatever we choose to focus on and pursue. "Thoughts become actions, actions become habits and habits become our destiny,"[15] according to Global Priority Solutions.

Dear Lord,
    Praise You, Father. Thank you for filling me with Your loving kindness. Forgive me for replacing You with this relationship. I give You this

relationship with a very dear friend, Lord. I trust You and choose not to be reliant on it anymore. It's hard, Lord. Thank You for the strength to overcome. Teach me and thank you for filling me with Your love and the fruit of the Spirit so I may be a shining light for You in everything I say and do.

Praise You, Lord. I trust You. Thank You for giving me joy and excitement about what You have in store for my life. Thank You, Lord, for Your everlasting love. Teach me how to love myself through You, Lord, and to find myself beautiful. Amen

CHAPTER 10

Will I Ever Be Enough?

Do you ever feel like you are not enough? The good news is that you are enough. You are complete in Him. (Colossians 2:10 NKJV) Through Jesus Christ, our Lord and Savior, who died on the cross, suffering beating, scoffing, spitting, whipping, and derisive laughter. He went through all of that for us. He was the perfect sacrifice who died in our place so that we could be free from all shame, blame, and guilt, so we could be made righteous and have a glorious life through Him. He is the way, the truth, and the life. Without Him, we have no life. I'm talking about the kind of life that is full of joy and fulfillment, the life where we can have as much of Jesus as we want. We cannot be perfect without Him, for He is the way to a perfect life.

> *He is* the Rock, His work *is* perfect; For all His ways *are* justice, A God of truth and without injustice, Righteous and upright *is* He.
>
> —Deuteronomy 32:4 (NKJV)

Because of my attitude toward the sins I had committed, I didn't think I could control my thoughts. I believed the lie that I was not worthy to be loved by anyone because my thinking was unclear, still full of shame, blame, and guilt. I hadn't forgiven myself. I felt I deserved more punishment for my sins, even though Jesus died and took care of all of that for me. I didn't understand that enormous act of love when God sent His Son as the ultimate sacrifice for all of our sins: past, present, and future.

When I was looking for answers, I asked God, "Am I behaving in a proper manner, or am I misbehaving?" At those times, I already knew the answer. I was searching for answers from God to justify my sin. I wanted permission to go and feed my selfish desires, yet another part of me wanted to know, "If I am really disobedient, will you still love me? God, will you love me enough to stop me from what I am about to do?" When He didn't stop me, I understood that response to mean He was giving me permission. I didn't think about all the heartache my disobedience caused for everyone around me. I didn't care about everyone else; it was all about me.

When I had feelings of not being enough I became my own judge and played God. No one had to punish me—I did a fine job all by myself. I would create negative situations in my own mind, so I wouldn't be surprised when something negative did happen. Because of my past experiences (when I didn't deal with those negative encounters or work through those unwholesome emotions), I chose to suppress my emotions so I didn't have to look at all the ugliness I felt. Those hideous emotions began to surface, and I continued with my "stinking thinking" instead of renewing my mind and stopping the negative thoughts as soon as they entered the door of my mind.

> *As for* God, His way *is* perfect; The word of the Lord is proven; He *is* a shield to all who trust in Him.
>
> —Psalm 18:30 (NKJV)

As we seek God and His ways, instead of reacting to what people say or do out of anger, loneliness, resentment, feeling not enough or wanting to be right, we can talk to the Holy Spirit. When we talk to Him as we would our best friend. He will guide us in the right direction and will never lead us astray. His ways are faithful and true, and the more we practice what the Word says, the more following Him becomes second nature to us. He is a shield to us when we trust Him. He makes everything turn out for good, even if it started out badly. He is amazing.

When we begin to trust God, peace comes. Whenever we notice that we are feeling anxious, we can stop and pray. Praying can look a lot of different ways, we can pray anytime, anywhere. For example: to say a prayer in our mind while we are talking to someone, walking down the street, riding a bike, driving the car, or swimming. Pray about everything. The more we talk to God, He will bring to remembrance the things we have learned, and His amazing peace will wash over us. When we notice we're not in peace, it is easy to get back in. All we have to do is focus on what He has told us in His Word. (Philippians 4:6-7) Have faith and believe exactly what the Word of God says about who you are.

We are created in God's image; therefore, we are complete when we are living and striving to be like Jesus, living every detail in our lives in love. Love does make the world go around. When we deal with conflicts in love, when we talk to people in love, we can watch and see how our world changes around us.

Every situation we encounter can become a teaching moment. Even if we didn't handle it well, we can ask the Holy Spirit what we could have done differently to have a positive, loving outcome, and He will show us. Even if we don't get a second chance with the same person, we will have another chance for a "do over" which will allow an opportunity to succeed in a more gratifying, loving way that produces positive fruit.

When we think we have to accomplish these tasks all by ourselves, we must think again. God is with us every step of the way, and if we ask Him to give us the words, we can thank Him for getting us through the area where we are feeling weak. We will be amazed by His strength as he completes the task. He is always there, and we only need to ask for help. He does the rest.

Hallelujah! We are alive in Him. We are made complete in Him. When we are feeling lonely and in search of love and acceptance, we seek Him, for He is the one whom we crave. No man/woman alive can fill us up as Jesus can. As we surrender every thought, emotion, and doubt to Him, He will fill us to overflowing.

Having God in our lives on a daily basis is the most fulfilling experience, for He will never leave us nor forsake us, and He will not make fools of us. When we ask Him a question, He answers us since He is always fully alert and listening to us. He will guide us into all truth and will bring to remembrance everything He has taught us. How cool is that? He sticks closer than a brother.

I came across *The Reason for God* by Tim Keller, who says:

> "An identity based on God also leads inevitably to deep forms of addiction. If we take our meaning in life from our family, our work, as cause, or some

achievement other than God, they enslave us. We have to have them… As in all addiction, we are in denial about the degree to which we are controlled by our god-substitutes. And inordinate love creates inordinate, uncontrollable anguish if anything goes wrong with the object of our greatest hopes."[16]

Frank Outlaw offers these words of wisdom:

Watch your thoughts for they become words; watch your words because they become actions, and watch your actions for they become habits. Watch your habits because they become your character; watch your character because it becomes your destiny.[17]

God has given us the gifts, talents, abilities, and grace we need to do His will in life. God's grace is actually His power, and He will not only give us grace but promises grace and more grace in James 4:6. He never runs out of power—and His power is available to us. If we don't keep the right mindset, the enemy can defeat us with thoughts of inadequacy, but if we make up our mind that we can do what we need to do, we'll find that we can do anything—not in our own strength but in the strength God gives us. "I can do all things through Christ who strengthens me." (Philippians 4:13) We must keep our minds filled with peace, balance, discipline, and self-control. Begin each day by saying, "I can do whatever I need to do in life through Christ."

Test the Spirits

It seems like whenever we ask ourselves, "Will I ever be enough?" the enemy likes to make us feel defeated. But he can only be successful if we give Him power, Satan is like a mouse with a megaphone. He makes us think he is big and tough, but he has absolutely no power unless we give it to him. Always "test the spirits."

> Beloved, do not believe every spirit, but test the spirits, whether they are of God; because many false prophets have gone out into the world. By this you know the Spirit of God: Every spirit that confesses that Jesus Christ has come in the flesh is of God, and every spirit that does not confess that Jesus Christ has come in the flesh is not of God. And this is the *spirit* of the Antichrist, which you have heard was coming, and now already in the world.
>
> —1 John 4:1–3 (NKJV)

God's Word is our sword against the enemy. When Jesus walked on this earth and was tempted by Satan, He used the Word to defeat him. We can do the same. When those negative thoughts challenge us—whether in the areas of health, finances, fear, doubt, insecurity, anger, or depression—we go to the Word and ask God to reveal to us what we need to know, and He will guide us and direct us.

Just as God instilled confidence in David, who believed he could slay Goliath, He places a similar sense of knowing in us, providing us with all the armor we need in Ephesians 6 when we encounter spiritual battles. We only have to seek Him and believe we can do all things through Christ who strengthens us, and God will personally direct us in the way we ought to go. His Word is our weapon against everything. For this crucial reason, we must stay in His Word daily, to keep our relationship with Him strong and to seek Him before we face any giants.

Write your thoughts and God's answers in a journal. Repeat His Word over and over until you have defeated all negative thinking. Continually repeat this practice until it becomes a habit. Negative thinking can always creep into our thoughts, but if we are in the habit of kicking them out every time they enter, they cannot gain any power over us. When we let doubt and fear creep into our lives, they weaken us. God is a God of life and confidence, not fear. As we read His word, we believe it, live it and breathe it. We allow it to work for us as a sword to win this battle in our mind. God is faithful.

Every morning, put on the full armor of God found in Ephesians 6:10–18.

Will I Ever Be Enough?

Dear Heavenly Father,

Thank You for this day. Thank You for giving me victory over_____. (Name what you are battling.) As I go through this day, Lord, I put on the full armor of God so that I can stand against the devil's schemes. For my struggles are not against flesh and blood, but against the rulers, against the authorities, against the powers of this dark world and against the spiritual forces of evil in the heavenly realms.

Therefore, I put on the full armor of God, so that when the day of evil comes, I may stand my ground, and after I have done everything to stand, I will stand firm, having girded my waist with truth, having put on the breastplate of righteousness, and having shod my feet with the preparation of the gospel of peace. Above all, I take up the shield of faith, with which I will be able to quench all the fiery darts of the evil one, and the helmet of salvation and the sword of the Spirit, which is the Word, praying always with all prayer and supplication in the Spirit.

Thank You that He Who is in me is greater than he that is in the world. (1John 4:4) And we know that nothing can penetrate this armor. Thank You, Lord, for the precious gift of Your Word; it teaches me in time of meditation and helps me in time of trouble. Thank You, Lord, that I may encourage someone today and be uplifting and edifying to glorify Your name.

In Jesus' holy name, Amen.

CHAPTER 11

Whose Life Is This Anyway?

Do you feel as if everyone is always telling you what to do and how to live your life? Some people say our behavior is absolutely correct while other people say our actions are totally improper. Whom are we to believe? We get tossed this way and that way. Some people say, "Go ahead and satisfy your emotional needs. If it feels good, do it." Others say, "If you follow those impulses, you will be struck by lightning." Someone seeking an extramarital relationship might say, "We have an open marriage." What does an "open marriage" mean? And who made up all these different rules?

Opinions range from giving people a piece of our mind to thinking all of our opinions are valid and we have a right to tell people how to live their lives. We do have the right to our own opinion, but it isn't always the best time to share it. The Holy Spirit will let us know when the proper time arrives or if we need to keep our opinions to ourselves. He will guide us into all truth while we attempt to justify everything to validate our behavior about anything we decide to do. It is wise to check with the Holy Spirit by seeking Him in prayer, asking Him for His opinion, and reading His Word.

Our lives belong to each of us, and we create our own way of life however we choose, but when we partner with Jesus, there is more adventure, excitement, and amazement than we can obtain from anything in this entire universe. His promises are true and everlasting. No matter what area we want to involve Him, He is faithful to guide us. He turns what seems to be ordinary into the most exciting event. As we look back on our lives, we can see evidence of where He carried us through and provided wonderful opportunities for us: He saved us from danger or helped us sell our house or car. He opened doors for us to get a job and put people in our lives to help us. The list goes on.

Seeking God When We Feel Offended

When circumstances don't go the way we think they ought to, or a good friend puts us down or talks behind our back, it can be hurtful.

When we don't know what to do after feeling as if someone mistreated us, specifically our spouse, we may begin thinking of having an affair or getting a divorce. If our spouse has been unfaithful, or whatever our circumstance may be, and we want to get even or show them how it feels, we need to stop!

We want to give them a piece of our mind, but acting out of anger and hurt is not a good way to talk it out with them. Instead, first talk to God about it. He is our Rock; the Holy Spirit will help us see the truth. His ways are perfect, and as we work it out with Him, He helps us see a new perspective. He will give us the right words at the right time. He will help us see why the offense hurt us and show us the root cause of it.

More than likely, if we are considering revenge or unfaithfulness, the last thing we want to do is talk to God about it. But instead of moving away from God, we must seek Him more, for He has the answers we are looking for. He can help us see more clearly by showing us the truth about the situation. He can even turn the circumstances around and noticeably improve the entire situation. Pray ahead of time and talk to God about your weaknesses.

Amazingly, I could quickly forget about God and His promises, but He will never leave me or forsake me. Yet I blamed Him for all kinds of challenging circumstances that I did not care about resolving. Looking back, I now ask myself, "Did you pray about it first? Did you ask God for His opinion? Did you listen to Him when He warned you in advance, or did you brush Him off like a pesky fly?" Not only did He warn me about the way I wanted to proceed with my own offense, or nudge me that my thinking was not in line with His Word once, but more than likely three or four times until I blocked His warnings altogether and went ahead and did as I pleased. When we ignore His warnings, we will become immune to that tug we feel and think our way is better.

After 15 years of marriage, I finally realized that I was seeking myself for the answers, I surrendered and ask God to help me work through my wounded heart. I began to challenge any negative thoughts that tried to enter my mind. I would talk to God. I even asked Him to please not let a certain person come into our presence because I couldn't handle it that day. To my amazement, they left, and I thanked God for blessing me. Because I obeyed Him and didn't entertain the thought and sought His guidance, He helped me. He will not tempt you beyond what you are able to bear.

I am here to advise you that if you find yourself at a crossroads, ask yourself, "What is the real motive for moving forward in this situation, and how will it impact all the people involved? Is it a win-win for all parties?" You may find that your friends will encourage you to follow through in a matter, but you have to ask yourself if they are *really* good friends. The world says, "If it feels good, do it." The enemy may tell us, "You only live once. You will be missing out on this if you don't go for it." This battle is real, and Satan is only out to steal, kill and destroy us and everything around us.

When we fix our eyes on Jesus, we must quote His truths until they sink in or until the negative feelings shift into positive responses. Otherwise, our lives become like prison cells we create for ourselves, and we believe we can't get out, yet all we have to do is open the door and walk out to the freedom God has said we already have when we accept Him. We make life so difficult when it is so easy. Who told us life was hard anyway?

What is controlling you?

Cheating on a diet is like sin—we know how it affects our mind, body, and soul When we indulge in food that is not good for us, yet we eat it anyway. As soon as we decide we are going to go on a diet, all of a sudden, we want to eat everything we told ourselves we can't have.

We go through different stages in our mind when we first decide to modify our usual routine, such as changing our diet. We can become addicted to life habits, such as the food we choose to eat, and we can rebel and refuse to change. When we first hear new information, we may attempt to digest it while making excuses and telling ourselves, "I don't need to change. It's not that bad for me," or "I'm not that overweight" or "Maybe that's not for me. I like my food, and I like my life." All the while, in our minds there is an urgent need to change. We start to do more research, read labels and examine any material we can find as to how this diet is going to improve our lives. We start to justify that our plan of action is just as beneficial as the plans of everyone else.

One day I decided to eliminate every unhealthy food item from my life. The first week, I was excited and did well, but the second week I found this practice was more difficult than I thought. The third week rolled around, and temptation started to enter my thoughts. I said, "A little of this won't hurt," as I partook of a small amount or told myself a little white lie, that it didn't hurt anything to have one bite. I found I wanted a little bit more, and it became easier and easier as I began to slide back into my old habits, and then the rebellion came. "I'm going to eat anything I want; I only live once, and I'm going to have it all." The urgent thoughts would not go away, but now they were about my choice to go ahead and indulge. The cycle repeated itself over and over again until I got tired of the same results. My struggle with sin was a similar cycle to that of dieting.

What can we do to stay free?

We can pray ahead of time and imagine ourselves being the persons we want to be and not caving under peer pressure. Stay strong in the Lord. We must associate with a friend or friends who will encourage us to keep on the right path and avoid friends who want to make us feel guilty or those who encourage us that what we were doing wasn't hurting anything.

We must focus on the end results—positive pictures of who we want to be—as we focus on our relationship with Jesus. When we let Jesus direct our lives we will start seeing ourselves successful as we step into a life of wholeness.

CHAPTER 12

I Am Grateful for You

God's promises and covenants are true and just.

"My covenant I will not break, Nor alter the word that has gone out of My lips. Once I have sworn by My holiness; I will not lie to David: His seed shall endure forever, And his throne as the sun before Me; It shall be established forever like the moon, Even *like* the faithful witness in the sky."

—Psalms 89:34–37, NKJV

We were all put on this earth to serve God, our Father, and we ought to be grateful that we get to serve Him with a cheerful heart. We are born selfish, however, wanting everything our own way, doing everything to make sure whatever we do benefits us, and when it doesn't, anger, bitterness, envy, resentment, and jealousy all come as a result.

We have the power to change our own lives positively or negatively. We work hard and exhaust ourselves, seeking fulfillment by creating a perfect environment, but we always fall short in our efforts. It doesn't matter how much fulfillment we find, how much money we spend, or how many friends we have, there is still a void that we cannot always identify. No matter what we do, this inner yearning for more doesn't change with time. It doesn't change how we feel. We get frustrated because we can't make the money come in more quickly. Time moves too slowly for our circumstances to adjust.

The only thing we are in control of is our attitude toward every event that comes our way. We can look at the event with a grateful heart and be positive, having hope that everything is going to work out exactly as God intended. We get to choose how long our journey in the desert will be or the attitude we will have while going through it. Jesus says He is the way, the truth, and the life. Why do we ever doubt that?

Believe

At times we get stuck in our cycles of life and wonder why God isn't doing anything, but He has given us everything we need. "Everything is within you now," says Lance Wallnau.[18] God sent His Son, Jesus, to die on the cross for us, and He died and rose again on the third day. He sent the Holy Spirit to live and dwell in every one of us to guide us and give us direction. That is why we must pray without ceasing and listen to His advice.

The Word is our instruction manual for every trial and temptation and every conceivable offense we can think of. Everything has already been done, going back to when God created the world, and He has told us exactly how to handle it. He says not to worry, so why do we? He says He takes care of all our needs, so why do we doubt? He is an abundant God who didn't make this planet with shortages. He is a great planner and takes care of every need we have. We get to choose if we are going to let Him be our protector and provider. We can trust Him to do what He says. He has already gone before us and has outlined everything. He knows us and knows all. He has provided everything we need.

When trials and temptations come and we have accepted Jesus into our hearts, we have the Holy Spirit who teaches us everything we need to know. He guides us and directs our paths, and we have the mind of Christ (1 Corinthians 3:13–17). When Satan tempted Jesus after

He'd been fasting for forty days, He didn't rebuke him or cast him out; He spoke the Word to him. He spoke truth, combatting the twisted lies of the enemy. No one can argue with the Word. It is sharper than any two-edged sword and gets us out of every predicament we encounter (Hebrews 4:12). We get to believe what the Word says, and we have faith that what it says is true. We trust God to do the work and we stay out of His way so that He can. For that, I am eternally grateful.

How often do we seek the Word of God in perplexing situations? How satisfying life can be when we take the time every morning to seek God and read His Word. He gives us all the direction we need for that day. In our relationship with Him, He directs every path we ought to take. When something negative happens during the day and we reflect back to what we read and talked about with Father God in our quiet time, most assuredly we will receive what we were in need of.

When we make this practice our daily routine and we encounter situations where we don't feel as if we behaved properly, as we study the life of Jesus He shows us by example how to handle every situation that is presented. When we make a mistake we can reflect on how we could have handled it differently and what we learned from our mistake. As we practice, the right responses will start to come more naturally.

Have you ever noticed that if you are speeding while in your car, you may panic when a state trooper drives by? If you practice going the speed limit, you may still panic when you see a state trooper, but when you look at the odometer, you will notice that you are right on track. Because you have been practicing going the speed limit, following the law comes almost automatically. So it is with our lives-when we are following God fully. We need not panic when Satan rears his ugly head.

Another example of monitoring what we have been practicing is through our children. When we watch and listen to our children, they will give us a great indicator of how we act and talk because they imitate us, they walk, talk, and act like us. Jesus also said:

> "Therefore whoever humbles himself as this little child is greatest in the kingdom of heaven."
>
> —Matthew 18:4 (NKJV)

Children are also quick to forgive and eager to please and love us. Every circumstance in our lives is an opportunity for us to learn and to be more like Jesus. He gave us His Word to show us exactly how to live our lives to the fullest and to love and be loved. As circumstances present themselves with other people we can ask ourselves "What would Jesus do?"

According to the Wester's dictionary[19] the definition of monitor is one that admonishes, cautions or reminds. Which brings me to the scripture that says:

Then Jesus answered and said to them, "Most assuredly, I say to you, the Son can do nothing of Himself, but what He sees the Father do; for whatever He does, the Son also does in like manner.

—John 5:19 (NKJV)

A Grateful Heart

What is your passion? What are you focused on? I am a gardener, and I have always wanted to be a master gardener, but I have never actually taken the courses to get the certificate saying "I am a master gardener."

One summer, as I was gardening, I was focused on all the weeds in my garden. I went out every day and made sure my garden was weed-free. I imagined each new weed as a negative thought or a negative circumstance in my life, so I worked extra hard and was diligent to keep unwanted weeds out before they overran the garden. One day, I realized that I hadn't been harvesting any of my vegetables! As I was grumbling to God about my life and how I never got to do anything special for Him and how I wanted to be important, He very softly told me, "It is because you are so focused on the things you do wrong, the weeds in your life, that you never look at any of the fruit that I have given you." He also told me I am the master gardener of my own life, and I get to choose how healthy my garden will be. So I am a master gardener after all. I am grateful.

Spending Time with Jesus

I love to look at everything in my life as a lesson or a parable on what God is showing me. There is a miracle, a love note, a soft word of encouragement from Him all the time. If we take the time to spend with Him and trust Him, He is faithful. I am grateful for the words of Ryan Stevens: "NO MATTER WHAT YOU'VE DONE YOU CAN'T ERASE HIS LOVE." [20]

If we would put down our cell phone, shut off our television, and stay away from the internet, our ears would be more open to hear God speak to us. We could survive without these items for at least an hour a day. Just because our cell phone rings doesn't mean we have to answer it. When I have decided to practice this, I've noticed that is when the phone rings or something catches my eye on the television or the internet, and then I am distracted from going to spend that time with Jesus and may decide I'll put it off till tomorrow.

To spend time with Jesus, start with five minutes or even one verse and meditate on it. You will notice you will want more and more of Him, and pretty soon you can't get enough. When we let Him soothe our aches and pains instead of numbing ourselves with all of the world's stimulants, we become more filled with the fruit of the Spirit. You will only be grateful you did and wonder why you didn't do it sooner.

CHAPTER 13

The Greatest Love Affair

I have always sought men for acceptance, and the one man whom I thought was supposed to give me love and acceptance was my dad, and God took him from me (that has been the lie I have believed most of my life). In his place, He gave me my stepdad who, instead of giving me love and acceptance, rejected me and made me feel as if I was not worth anything. I sought love and acceptance by working diligently to impress him. I tried being well behaved as I attempted to be perfect, yet nothing I did was acceptable. In response to another lie I believed, I was always asking, "Who am I?" and "Why can't I do anything right? What is wrong with me?"

Seeking men to accept me and love me, I very carefully listened to their directions as to who they thought I should be. I picked men who wanted something from me or who wanted to change me because I didn't measure up to their standards just the way I was. As I tried to please them and go against being true to myself, I became very angry. My plans didn't work out. As I found myself searching for a breakthrough and still wondering who I was and blaming God for all of the people He had taken from me, I shielded my heart from loving anyone.

I never could understand why God wouldn't make people do what I wanted them to do or why they couldn't make me behave. I wanted Him to fix me and everyone else, and I wanted Him to fix them now.

I would seek His truth and then do the opposite. I found being obedient was too hard and boring and did not work for me. One day when I was deep in my crafty sin, I decided to draw near to God and really listen to His advice. I allowed Him to speak into my life, and He told me I had an addiction I didn't want to give up. I told Him "This guy is my friend, and you put him in my life. I don't want to give this relationship up because it will hurt too badly. I don't want to hurt anymore." Again, He told me, "There will be pain when the relationship dies. You get to mourn, and one day you won't feel pain but relief that you are no longer in bondage. One day you will realize the pain is not there anymore. "

"Okay, God. What if what Your Word says is true? You are the way, the truth, and the life. I am not to worry about anything; You have got my back. I am to pray about everything, and to pray without ceasing. I know that You are the Bread of Life, Living Water, the Light of the World, the Door of the Sheep, the Good Shepherd, the Resurrection and the Life, and the True Vine."

Soon I really did begin to listen to Him, now I am free of the lies I have believed that I need a man to make me feel good, to feel loved and cherished, and to be desirable and delighted in. Jesus is love, light, peace, joy, and kindness. He is merciful and forgiving. He is funny and exciting. He delights in me. When I started looking back over my life and paying attention to the times God showed up, I realized only the love of Jesus and my heavenly Father could have worked such miraculous transformations, which of course makes my heart swell with Joy when I realized how much He loves me.

Reflections

As I reflected back over my life and the choices I had made, I began to see how God had been there all along. The following story illustrations are of how God showed his love in my life:

There was a time when I thought I'd never get out of my first marriage. I was once told that everything I say will come to pass, so I'd better be careful what I say and what I wish for. I wished and spoke out almost every day that I was going to divorce Barrett, my first husband. I was abused and had become withdrawn and very insecure. As I was picking up my mail one day, some random lady said to me, "Life isn't that bad, is it?" She had no clue what I'd been through or the torment I lived daily.

It seems like every time I got the courage to leave my first marriage, I'd be pregnant again, (with Barrett's child) and felt like it was a sign from God to stay. I would feel frustrated, the hope of ever being free from the abuse of this relationship seemed hopeless. I hadn't worked since my daughter was a year old; she was now 10 years old, and my youngest of three children was two. There was a knock at my door on this particular day, I opened the door to a man who lived down the road from me. He asked me if I wanted a job at their office filing papers one day a week. He said he had been watching me transform the property that we lived on and all the work that I had done, and he would love to have me on their team. It sounded like a good idea, so I took the job.

A few months later when I was at the town office, the manager asked me if I wanted a job. He said all I had to do was fill out the application and come in for the interview. Although I was fearful, I applied and obtained the job. At that time, I was working two days a week and filling in for the manager on his days off. I was so afraid I was going to make a mistake and get in trouble. During the first three or four months, I didn't think I could handle it. As I persevered, however, I became more and more confident as I recognized my amazing ability to interact with people. God was slowly restoring my self-confidence.

I had been attending church regularly for about three years when Nancy moved to town from another state. She was really supportive of me and my children, she would babysit for me at no charge. She also provided support and informed me that the relationship I was in was not healthy and that I needed to get out of it. After about a year, she called and told me to be at her house because she had arranged for the police to be there and to escort me to a safe house. I was scared and didn't know if I could do that.

As always, Barrett showed up at the exact time I was getting ready to leave. When he asked where I was going, I started to cry and told him I had to go get some milk at the store. I told him I loved him as I took the children, put them in the car, and drove away. I was not going to miss this opportunity. I cried all the way to my friend's house, where the police met me and escorted me to a safe house 45 minutes away where I stayed for three days. During that time, another woman drove me to the courthouse and helped me obtain a restraining order, and everything seemed to fall in place. Barrett was ordered to get all of his belongings out of our house so I could return and safely live there.

After the divorce, I obtained the trailer house and the log addition attached to it. I could stay on the property as long as my now ex-husband agreed. On Christmas Eve two years after we divorced, I received a certified letter evicting my three children and me from the property. I had no idea where I was going or how I was going to do it, but I decided to sell the trailer. My trailer house was an older model, so the bank would not loan money on something that old, so anyone who wanted to buy it would have to have cash. The buyer would have to be a property owner outside the city limits because it was too old to be in a trailer park and was not allowed within the city limits. I was asking $4,000 for it. I received a call one day from a woman who was the perfect match. Although she loved the trailer, she wasn't thrilled about the log addition being attached to the side. She thought the small holes from the log bolts were unattractive, so she didn't want to buy it. I thought that ended all my chances to sell the trailer house.

A few weeks later, I received a call from a couple who also wanted to come look at it. They fell in love with it and said they'd be back with a check. A week later they came by with the check and made arrangements to have the trailer moved. I was so happy to get rid of it. The funny part of the story was that the people who bought it were working for the woman who first came to look at it and didn't want to buy it. When I saw that the check was from her and how God worked around her and used someone else to complete the task, I knew then that God was taking care of me. I always loved to hear how God worked in people's lives and performed miracles, and now I had my own story to tell.

After three years, I was safe and getting ready to marry my second husband when Nancy whom God had placed in my life seemed to have vanished. She had given me some of her belongings and moved away, and I had not heard from her. I believe she was an angel whom God placed in my life to help me escape from the trap where I had so carelessly placed myself. At the same time, another one of my dear friends whom I relied on for support moved away, and she gave me all of her cleaning jobs. I am so thankful, and now I can see how God took care of me mentally, physically, financially, and relationally. He is a loving God who makes all things work together for the good for those who love Him.

As I look back at my life, I see all the times I tried to self-protect, self-provide, and control every area of my life. I also recognize the different ways I became addicted to circumstances in search of love and acceptance. I discovered that to be addicted to Jesus and His love is greater than any high this world offers; there is none like it. My relationship with Him is the greatest love affair I have ever had. He shows me I am loved. He is always there when I need Him. He never leaves me or forsakes me. He never shames me. I can tell Him everything that comes to mind, every evil desire that crosses my mind, and He shows me exactly what I must to do. He is the most wonderful Father I could have ever imagined. He loves me no matter what I have done.

All my life He has been calling to me with His arms open wide, saying, "Come to me, my child, and rest in Me." So many times I would tell Him, "I can do this myself," but He would say, "I will be here when you are ready."

He is also waiting for you with open arms. Give Him a chance, and you will not regret it. His promises are true. You, too, are the heir of the one true King; you are royalty. We have a Father who loves us and adores us. He delights in us. He only wants what is good for us, and He wants to protect us. He fills us with love, joy, peace, long-suffering, kindness, goodness, faithfulness, gentleness, and self-control (Galatians 5:22).

> Cause me to hear Your lovingkindness in the morning, For in You do I trust;
> Cause me to know the way in which I should walk, For I lift up my soul to You.
> Deliver me, O Lord, from my enemies; In You I take shelter. Teach me to do Your will,
> For You *are* my God; Your Spirit *is* good. Lead me in the land of uprightness.
> Revive me, O Lord, for Your name's sake! For Your righteousness' sake bring my soul out of trouble. In Your mercy cut off my enemies, And destroy all those who afflict my soul; For I *am* Your servant.
>
> —Psalm 143:8–12(NKJV)

Who I Am

I am who I am only because of the love of the Lord Jesus Christ, not because of religion but because of the awesome relationship I have with Him. He has been the Father I never had, and He has comforted me in all those times I needed to be loved. He is always there for me as long as I am willing to let Him in and accept and hear what He has to say. If I try to do anything on my own, thinking I need to be in control of the outcome of any situation, I miserably fail. Yet, when I bring everything before my Father in heaven, it always works out when I listen.

The joy I feel inside every day is the love of God shining through me. I used to be selfish, prideful, angry, and a hateful person. I can still have all of those traits if I choose to let my humanity take over. "Create in me a pure heart, O God, and renew a steadfast spirit in me," says Psalm 51:10. I don't claim to be perfect; my goal in life is to see people through the eyes of Jesus Christ. Wow! This attitude does make life exciting and fulfilling. I love Him with all my heart, mind, soul, and strength.

About The Author

Michelle Klaseen lives on a ranch in Western Colorado with her husband and their two youngest boys of 7 children. She has 6 grandchildren. She is dedicated to helping people break free from the torment that interferes with their lives. Through her writing, speaking, and coaching, she helps people identify with who they are in Christ and gives her readers tools to help move them forward to a positive life of freedom.

Michelle has struggled with her own confidence of who she is through mental and physical abuse. She has also suffered through shame, blame, and guilt while searching for love, acceptance, and validation while enduring eating disorders, adultery, and addiction. She is now a transformed woman full of love, hope, and living a life of abundant joy through her Savior, Jesus Christ. She helps others to become free from the lies they believe and to spring into a life of hope and love.

Endnotes

1. Thompson, Adam F., and Adrian Beale. *The Divinity Code to Understanding Your Dreams and Visions.* Shippensburg. PA: Destiny Image, 2011
2. "Meaning & Symbolism of Lilac." Daffodil/Narcissus Flower Meanings & Symbolism | Teleflora. Accessed March 08, 2019. https://www.teleflora.com/meaning-of-flowerslilac
3. "Color Meanings-All About Colors and symbolism." Color-Meanings.com. Accessed March 7, 2019. https//www.colors-meanings.com/.
4. Webster's II New College Dictionary. Boston: Houghton Mifflin, 1995.
5. Wright Henry W., and Henry Wright. *A More Excellent Way to Be in Health.* New Kensington, PA: Whitaker House, 2009

6. Meyer, Joyce, writer, *Joyce Meyer*-Attitudes of the heart, Joyce Meyer Ministries, 2005, Audio Teaching
7. Meyer, Joyce, writer, *Joyce Meyer*-Attitudes of the heart. Joyce Meyer Ministries, 2005, Audio Teaching
8. Meyer, Joyce, writer, *Joyce Meyer*- Attitudes of the heart, Joyce Meyer Ministries, 2005, Audio Teaching
9. Webster's II New College Dictionary. Boston: Houghton Mifflin, 1995
10. Eddie Espinosa, a counselor @ Orange CA High School
11. Author Unknown
12. Meyer Joyce Battlefield of the Mind Overcome Negative thoughts and Change Your Mind, London; Hodder and Stoughton, 2008
13. Meyer, Joyce, writer, *Joyce Meyer*, Attitudes of the heart, Joyce Meyer Ministries, 2005, Audio Teaching
14. Meyer Joyce Battlefield of the Mind Overcome Negative thoughts and Change Your Mind. London; Hodder and Stoughton, 2008 Keyword You can even justify the behaviors and dress them up as spiritual.
15. Quote investigator: the earliest evidence of closely matching expression located by QI was published in a Texas newspaper feature called "What They're Saying" in May 1977. The saying was ascribed to the creator of a successful U.S. supermarket chain called Bi-Lo: 1977 May 18, San Antonio Light, What They're Saying, Quote Page 7-B(NArch Page 28), Column 4, San Antonio, Texas. (Newspaper Archive.)

[16] Keller Timothy. The Reason for God: Belief in an Age of Skepticism. Riverhead Books, 2008, Page 172

[17] Outlaw, Frank, Late President of the Bi-Lo Stores, 1977 May 18, San Antonio Light, What They're Saying, Quote Page 7-B (NArch Page 28) Column 4, San Antonio, TX (Newspaper Archive).

[18] Wallnua, Lance. In a Heartbeat, By Lance Wallnau

[19] Webster's II New College Dictionary. Boston: Houghton Mifflin, 1995

[20] Stevenson, Ryan "NO MATTER WHAT." In No Matter What. Ryan Stevenson (feat. Bart Millard of MercyMe) CD

www.ingramcontent.com/pod-product-compliance
Lightning Source LLC
LaVergne TN
LVHW011832060526
838200LV00053B/3984